Jacques Stroumsa   Violinist in Auschwitz

Jacques Stroumsa

<u>Violinist in Auschwitz</u>

From Salonica to Jerusalem
1913 – 1967

**Translated from German
by James Stewart Brice**

**Edited
by Erhard Roy Wiehn**

**Hartung-Gorre Verlag
Konstanz**

Front cover photo : Jacques Stroumsa 1945, back cover photo 1995 (photo Wiehn)
Reprint of the first edition 1996 in 2019 by Books on Demand (BoD), Norderstedt

Bibliographic information published by Die Deutsche Nationalbibliothek

Die Deutsche Nationalbibliothek lists this publication in the Deutsche Nationalbibliografie; detailed bibliographic data is available in the internet at http://dnb.ddb.de.

First edition 1996
HARTUNG-GORRE VERLAG, KONSTANZ (Germany)
http://www.hartung-gorre.de
ISBN-10: 3-89191-869-0
ISBN-13: 978-3-89191-869-2

Contents

Dedication

During my two years as a prisoner in Nazi death camps I was a witness to acts of unimaginable cruelty. At that time I decided that should I emerge from this inferno, I would report on everything that happened to me. Finally the time has come; it is late, but not too late. Perhaps it is actually just the right time.

This little book of memories would probably never have been finished without the constant, loving support of my wife, Laura. She herself, at the time just eighteen years old, suffered through a year in the concentration camp Bergen-Belsen. She also bears permanent wounds from her experiences. In memory of her parents she has nevertheless persevered and remained loyally at my side.

It was my good fortune to have made the acquaintance of Barbara Weil. Thanks to her valuable advice a text was finally completed. Finally, it should be mentioned that since our work together in Yad Vashém, a warm friendship has bound me together with Brigitte Pimpl. She acquainted me with Professor Wiehn, who was willing to edit the text and publish the book in Germany and undertook to make the German translation[1]*. I thank them all from the bottom of my heart.

This text is dedicated to the memory of all those who never returned.

---

* This dedication was written for the German edition. The text was originally written in French by Jacques Stroumsa and then translated into German by Brigitte Pimpl. It was edited and prepared for publication by Professor Erhard Roy Wiehn. The English text is a translation from the German by an American. Thus it is truly an example of international cooperation! For helping me revise the English translation, I wish to thank Roberta Chester.

Jacques Stroumsa: Preface to the English edition

Professor Dr. Erhard Roy Wiehn from the University of Konstanz and editor of an important collection of books about the Shoáh, has asked me to write a preface for the English edition of my book, Violinist in Auschwitz. The experience acquired in Germany during my lectures at Gymnasia (high schools) in Berlin and neighboring Potsdam in 1993 and 1994 gave me a number of important insights which I would like to share with the English-speaking public. The Nazi concentration camps were intended to completely destroy the human personality and to reduce it to a number tattooed on the skin, like animals in a slaughterhouse. The questions that people asked were, for example: having survived physically after being in Auschwitz and Mauthausen for two years, having survived the terrible Death March in January 1945, how did you find the strength to be a human being again; how did you adjust to living in a normal society again? Above all, where did you find the strength to come back to Germany (the land where crime was so scientifically organized) and, day after day, tell young Germans the details of your sufferings? How could you tell them that the younger generation is not guilty, that they and their parents (who are now the same age as my children) were not even born at the time when these events occurred? The answers to these anguished questions were given to me by the children themselves; they were deeply moved by my lectures. - One day, in December 1994, I received an invitation from Micaela von Marcard, head dramaturge of the Berlin State Opera, to attend the Memorial Concert to be given in Berlin on January 28, 1995, on the fiftieth anniversary of the liberation of Auschwitz. Also, Mrs. von Marcard asked me to write some „Memories of Auschwitz" for Vivace, the bulletin of the State Opera. I used the occasion of my visit to Berlin to present several lectures at various Gymnasia in the vicinity and, most important, to once again meet a few of the girls who had written to me after my original lectures. - I am very grateful to Mr. and Mrs. Leonhard Dünnwald for organizing this reunion in their villa in Berlin. I am also very grateful to four girls, Juliana, Tina, Katrin and Kristin for coming so far to our meeting and for their most thoughtful contributions to the discussions of these very anguished questions. - My sincere appreciation to James S. Brice, an American student at the University of Konstanz, for translating from German. He gave me the opportunity to reach the English-speaking public directly. - Finally, my warmest gratitude to my beloved wife, Laura, who never ceases to encourage me in the fight for this noble cause.
    Jerusalem and Tiberias, April 1, 1995.

'Valley of the destroyed communities' Yad Vashem, Jerusalem

Erhard Wiehn: Preface to the English edition

On April 29, 1940, Reichsführer SS Heinrich Himmler issued the order to build the concentration camp Auschwitz I, near the Polish town of Oswiecim, thirty miles west of Cracow. In September 1941 the Nazis experimented with killing using gas, and in the summer of 1942, four modern gas chambers were put into operation, alongside their respective crematoria.

On May 8, 1943, Jacques Stroumsa and his entire family: parents, his pregnant wife and aunts, uncles, cousins, etc., entered Auschwitz-Birkenau after an exhausting transport from Salonica, Greece. When it was evacuated on the evening of January 21, 1945, he left Auschwitz without a single member of his family (one sister survived the Holocaust). On January 25, 1945, he arrived at the camp Mauthausen, east of Linz/Danube in Austria, where he was liberated by American soldiers on May 8, 1945. The Red Army liberated Auschwitz on January 27, 1945, after 1.6 million people had been murdered there, most of them Jewish men, women and children. - I first met Dr. Jacques Stroumsa in Konstanz, in the autumn of 1992, on the occasion of his autobiographical lecture. In the spring of 1993 we could begin working on the text of his memories. At the beginning of August, still much impressed by my first visit to the Holocaust Memorial Museum in Washington, D.C., I wrote the foreword „Reporting About Auschwitz." The book *Violinist in Auschwitz* appeared in German during the fateful month of November 1993. About one year later, James Stuart Brice, an American student at the University of Konstanz who had been familiar with my publications on the subject for some time, graciously offered to translate the book into English. His proposition, of course, was gratefully accepted. Many thanks also to Prof. Dr. Morten Nøjgaard (Odense Universitet, Denmark) for proof reading and especially to Allison Wetterlin (University of Konstanz).

This publication is also appropriate in 1996, a year after the fiftieth anniversary of the end of the Second World War. In many countries of the world, especially England, France, Poland, Holland, Belgium, and certainly Israel, numerous ceremonies were held to commemorate this event. As the years pass and the Holocaust recedes further and further into the collective memory, eyewitness reports will become more and more precious. Jacques Stroumsa's *Violinist in Auschwitz* is an important contribution to our struggle against forgetfulness. We are grateful he has recorded his memories for posterity.

Konstanz, January 27, 1996

An hour

for Jacques Stroumsa,
Violinist in Auschwitz

Time must keep silent, today,
faced with the truth of your yesterday,
faced with the fear of a tomorrow,
that it will find.
A great cry echoes silently
in your:
WHY

Time stands still, today,
frozen by your words,
broken by their burden,
timeless and silent.
One question and many reproaches
in your:
WHY

Time must go on, today,
just as it did not die because of yesterday,
branded by the truth
against forgetfulness.
It must cry, every hour,
for us:
AUSCHWITZ

Juliane Kunze, Neuenhagen, January 28, 1995 (Translated from German by Mrs.
Karola Dünnwald)

Jacques Stroumsa

Writing down memories

One day in May 1970, while I was at work in my office, the telephone rang. My secretary, Hanna Ofri, widowed in the Six Days War of 1967 and intensely loyal to me, called, „Teddy's secretary would like to speak with you!" I learned that in ten minutes I was expected to be in the office of Teddy Kollek, the Mayor of Jerusalem. „Good heavens," I thought, „and what if I had been out?" - Our office at 10 Shamai Street was a mere ten minutes on foot from Teddy Kollek's office, provided that one didn't meet anyone on the way. At the time I still did not know that many people in Jerusalem, but many knew who I was. And everyone asked for help: This one needed a street light installed in front of his house, another wanted one for the street in front of his best friend's house, and a rabbi had been waiting a long time for the entrance to his synagogue to receive the needed illumination or asked for something for a colleague. Naturally that took time, and Teddy did not like it when someone came too late.

By chance, I managed to arrive without incident. The secretary said, as usual, „Go in, he is already waiting!" In Israel people do not shake hands when they meet. Teddy graciously introduced me to a visitor, „Stroumsa is my expert for public lighting, and he will do everything that you request!" Then he turned to me and remarked, „Surely you know Elie Wiesel, the famous author, like you a survivor of the concentration camps. He has a very urgent problem, but he can explain that to you better himself. In any case, see to it that you satisfy him just as if you were working for me!" - We went out to the stairs. I was a bit excited to be standing so suddenly alone with Elie Wiesel. „Do you have a car?" he asked directly in French. - „No, I came on foot, my office is fairly close." - „Then come with me, I will explain why I am here in Jerusalem!" - Elie Wiesel had, at that time, not yet received the Nobel Peace Prize (1986), but he was already a very well known personality. I had read several of his books and thus knew who he was, but was silent at first. - We arrived at the great square before the Tomb of David. Elie Wiesel explained to me, „On this site I am supposed to photograph a few scenes for a film to be paid for by an American firm. I need a lot of light, very powerful projectors; all costs will go on our account - workers, material, etc. But everything must be ready within forty-eight hours!" We climbed back into his car, and he let me off in the vicinity of my office with the words, „If there be any problems, call me at the 'King David'. I'm counting on you!"

I studied my plans and determined that there was no electrical outlet at the place designated by Elie Wiesel, not a single lamppost in the vicinity of King David's Tomb. I immediately called my loyal foreman, Moshe Bouganim, and asked him to come as quickly as possible. I explained my dilemma. As we paced back and forth a bit helplessly on the square, we noted a high-tension transmission pole which stood about five hundred meters away. It belonged to the electric company. Moshe called to me, „You know the director well; go to him and ask for permission to tap this line!" - The center of Jerusalem is small enough so that everything can be reached quickly. I went at once to the electric company and asked to see the director. The secretary informed me graciously that I was already expected. Since his appointment, indissoluble ties of friendship bound me to the director, the engineer Paul Schefer. Lighting technique was his passion. He belonged to our group of lighting technicians in the framework of the Israeli Engineers' Organization and never passed up an opportunity to put his manifold resources at my disposal.

I explained my problem to him and gave him the number of the pole which I had noted down. Schefer said, „All well and good. It would be so simple if we weren't in the midst of a strike: I am naturally not allowed to do anything, and the strike could last at least two to three days!" When he saw how appalled I looked, however, he added, „I trust you enough, Stroumsa, to give you a confidential tip: With the proper precautions you can make a direct connection with our line yourself: Take a suitable transformer, do your work, and then afterward put everything back as it was!" - „But how can I pay for the electricity we use?" - „It will be my gift! But be careful, I have promised you nothing! You take responsibility for everything, and afterward you put everything back in its original condition, as if nothing had happened!" - I thanked Director Schefer warmly and, together with my foreman Moshe and his best worker, Rahamim Cohen, returned at once to our workplace. We worked twenty-four hours at a stretch. Two days later I called Elie Wiesel to inform him that everything was ready. He came with his team and openly displayed his great satisfaction. The spotlights were set up according to his instructions, and the scene was lighted „a giorno" (like daylight). The American team was able to film, and everything worked out as planned.

After completion of the job, Elie Wiesel asked me for the bill. Astonished at the modest amount, he added a few ten-dollar bills to it and informed me, „Tomorrow we are filming in the apartment of Golda Meir; I would like you to take over the electrical installation, and bring the appropriate projectors with you!" - Still accompanied by my excellent foreman Moshe, we began the necessary preparations to set up the electrical installation in the salon in which the interview was to take place. After Golda had greeted us, she took her seat in an easy chair, the inevitable cigarette in the corner of her mouth. Elie Wiesel sat at her side and the conversation was carried on with muted voices. It was hot, so during the break they served us cold drinks. Everything went excellently. After the session, Elie Wiesel thanked me and invited me to tea the next day in the 'King David'. - With a profoundly sad undertone in his voice, he asked me to tell about my life in the concentration camp. He listened quietly and did not interrupt for almost an entire hour. Finally he said, „Jacques, your story is touching, someone should write a book about it. Repeat everything for me on cassette, and I promise to make something of it!" - Dear Elie Wiesel, I ask for your forgiveness that I did not take your advice. I have often thought of it, but I also knew that with all your responsibilities and worldwide connections you would probably have no time to also think of my fate. Besides, I felt that no one but I could write down my memories of the deportation period.

A few years later, you were awarded the Nobel Prize. This honor to your extraordinary talents spread its radiance not only to the Jewish people, but especially to us in particular, the survivors of Auschwitz. You have understood better than anyone else how to keep the memory of our dead alive. And so you also came to the great auditorium of Yad Vashém, in order to share your thoughts with us. I, the one-time violinist of Auschwitz, was moved to tears. - Before I recount my story, I would like to present a poem originally written in Hebrew by Moshe Liba, an ambassador of Israel and also a talented painter, sculptor and poet. This poem was published at the request of the former President, Yitzak Navon, who wrote the foreword. He suggested translating it into eight different languages, including Yiddish, but above all, however, into Greek and Ladino, the violinist's mother tongue. - The poem was received with astonishing acclaim not only in various European countries, but also in Latin America as well. In Greece, the sculptor Evangelis Moustakas called it „a blow in the pit of mankind's stomach." In Chile, the author Enrique Lafourcade dedicated an entire page of his Santiago newspaper to it. In Lima, Miami and Jerusalem radio stations invited me to interviews in response to this poem. Whenever I speak at Yad Vashém or elsewhere on life in the concentration camps, I ask someone to read this poem before I speak, and it never fails to have a powerful effect on the audience. –

Jerusalem, March 1993

Moshe Liba

to Jacques-Jaakov Stroumsa
Survivor from Salonica

The violinist from Auschwitz

Every morning,
even when perchance
there was no nightmare
when I was not awakened
in a cold sweat
when I did not arise in fright
in terror of the SS.
Every single morning.

I ask myself
where shall I go today
I dress, drink tea,
start the car
and drive off -
where to?

The engine purrs
the sites rush by
the avenue, the traffic lights
the road leads up,
up the hill,
the open gate.
Every morning
Yad Vashém -
the Holocaust Memorial.

The same hum
the same voices
the same notes
the same music
the march
the little town in flames.
The music leads my car,
draws me like a magnet,

like a cable
like the chain of a winch
to Yad Vashém.

The Remembrance Tent
the Eternal Light
candles
the Hall of Names
the photos, eyes,
teeth, golden dentures, human hair.
Here are the gas chambers,
the furnaces
the crematoria
and Jews in striped, shapeless clothes
pushing bodies.
Naked women, trying in vain
to hide their shame
on the brink of the common grave.
Only the stench, the smoke and the music
are missing.

What means that noise,
the cadence of steps
„Links, left, left!"
The whip, the shots.
„Labor makes free"
on the arch above the gate.
And all around
walls, dogs, and barbed wire;
lists of names and numbers
and there is a hand - Yad, hands.
In the parade, who comes, who goes
where from, where to?

I played the violin there,
I was selected
for the orchestra
leading each day, in music,
the Jews driven
to the gas chambers
to the edge of the abyss
to the place from where
no one returns, no one comes back

is only removed, a corpse
to the incinerators.

No longer any need to run
no reason for fear
but this tune still turns round in my head.
And so, I will arrive,
here, today, yesterday,
tomorrow
in front of the musicians' photo:
an orchestra leading
the endless file of those who walk
in the Valley of the Shadow of Death.

Yes, I'm a grandfather now
my hair is white;
very little remains of me
but my features still resemble
a little bit, the fiddler, me,
there on the photo
from Auschwitz.

And yet it happens
that a visitor in Yad Vashém looks at me,
stare at the wall, and be stunned.
As if he saw one
from beyond the divide -
an apparition that, for him,
belongs to the other world;
that, for me, is
the world that was.

I will come here
morn by morn,
day by day,
with that music haunting me,
to the images on the wall
and to the stench in my nostrils
which only I can perceive.

This is my place, here I belong.
I am not a „living statue":
I live.

Of this monument
I am a part.
This Yad Vashém -
Hand and Name -
and body:
mine.

Erhard Roy Wiehn

Reporting once more about Auschwitz

Shouldn't this black chapter from the past finally be laid to rest? No, still anoth-er report must be given of Auschwitz and its barbarities. For no matter what we do, the past cannot be undone. What is written of it remains written. Everyone who wants to read of the past, can read. Everyone who wants to learn from it, can learn.

However, such a publication requires many fortunate circumstances. In the spring of 1992 Brigitte Pimpl, who lived not far from Konstanz, called me, of-fering to arrange a talk in Konstanz by a Dr. Jacques Stroumsa from Jerusalem, with whom, of course, I was at that time not yet acquainted. Since I knew Mrs. Pimpl fleetingly through an historian from Tel Aviv, after further telephone conversations I accepted her offer to make arrangements. In the summer of 1992, I invited Dr. Stroumsa to come to Konstanz that autumn to speak about „My Confinement at Auschwitz." The latter wrote to me on July 19, 1992 from Jerusalem, gratefully confirmed receiving my letter and wished to express his pleasure at the gracious invitation; he was looking forward with great interest to our meeting and the opportunity to speak with me about a few things, „I am sending you by special delivery an autobiographical sketch, an excerpt from the proceedings undertaken by the SS authorities against me for suspicion of at-tempted escape, and a copy of a poem dedicated to me by Moshe Liba, „The Fiddler from Auschwitz," in a German translation from the Hebrew original. I am well aware that the poem has more emotional than poetical significance. With very cordial greetings, Yours Stroumsa." I was very impressed; however, it hadn't occurred to me at that time that I would be able to help another victim to report about Auschwitz.

On Sunday, October 18, 1992, I met Dr. Jacques Stroumsa for the first time, shortly before his address, which was to take place in the framework of a mid-day meeting of the German-Israeli Society which fortunately was well attended. Just as I, after greeting the guests, had turned the podium over to him, he sur-prised me by graciously asking me to read aloud a poem by Moshe Liba - „The Fiddler from Auschwitz" - which I did, to be sure, even though this remarkable reading was very hard for me. After that Dr. Jacques Stroumsa spoke for barely an hour, rather softly and sometimes awkwardly, but without making a great fuss about the essential matter: his deportation from Salonica at the end of April 1943, his arrival at Auschwitz-Birkenau, the murder of his closest family members, his role as 'first violin' in the prisoners' orchestra of Auschwitz-Birkenau, his eventful 'stay' in Auschwitz, including his work in the 'Weichsel-Union Metal Works' of Auschwitz, the death march from Auschwitz to Mauthausen, his survival and his liberation. A look backward, today, reporting once more, fifty years later, on Auschwitz and other barbarities.

The next day we met for a longer discussion. Dr. Stroumsa had in the course of the years, admittedly, held many addresses, but previously had never published anything of great length on the story of his survival. For decades he had simply been unable to do this, quite apart from the fact that he thought that there was rather limited popular interest in it. In 1970 Elie Wiesel, then still not yet a Nobel Peace prize winner, had shown an interest in his story. But Jacques Stroumsa knew that he himself would have to write everything down, and that no one else could do this for him. For some time he had been working in Jerusalem on his life story, and now it was far enough along to start thinking of publication, which he wanted to entrust to me. Brigitte Pimpl's prompt agreement to translate the work from French into German and my spontaneous agreement to revise the text and publish it in my series, *Jewish Survival Fates*, seemed not merely to have pleased Jacques Stroumsa, but rather to literally have enthused him. At any rate his manuscript was finished much sooner than expected and was translated by Brigitte Pimpl, who personally gave me the text in mid-March 1993 in order to help report one more time on Auschwitz.

In fact, the author reports simply and authentically about atrocities which date back fifty years: about the destruction of the ancient Jewish community of Salonica, about suffering and death in concentration camp Birkenau, survival as a slave laborer of the German armaments industry in Auschwitz, even about the secret humanity of individual Germans who did not exactly feel themselves to be 'Aryan Masters' and about life after survival. For these survivors the past is, to be sure, as contemporary as though it happened yesterday. And yet it must be written down and published so that it will never be forgotten. Whether and what one can learn from these stories from history, whether eye-witness reports like this one will even be understood as a warning remains doubtful enough, if one thinks of the contemporary atrocities committed in former Yugoslavia and other places, and not least of all the serious developments in the new Germany. Documents like this should, however, at least make it harder - or, better still, help make it impossible - that anyone could ever again say that he had not known where hate and ethnic prejudice can lead. Therefore, another report about Auschwitz is still necessary.

This was certainly also a challenge for us, namely to make every effort to publish this survival story as soon as possible, which despite some difficulties we more or less succeeded in doing. The publication itself is, not least of all, thought of as a belated present on the occasion of its author's eightieth birthday. The fiftieth anniversary of his arrival at the German death camp Auschwitz-Birkenau took place on the 9th of May, 1993. Up until today he is reminded of this by the identification number, 121097, which is still visible, tattooed on his left forearm.

Even if those whom it most concerns have long since stopped wanting to hear about it: the truth remains the truth. Written down remains written down. Everyone who wants to read can read. Everyone who wants to learn from it can learn. Therefore it must be reported on once more, here about Auschwitz and other barbarities which can never be laid to rest.

Washington, D.C., August 10, 1993

Jacques Stroumsa
Violinist in Auschwitz

1. Family, childhood and youth in Salonica

Officially I was born in Salonica on January 4, 1913. The exact date of my birth is, however, not correctly entered in the official records, as all the archives of the Jewish community were lost in a terrible fire in 1917 which destroyed part of the city. Actually, I owe the recognition of this date by the French General Consulate to the testimony of two school comrades who were there as I signed the list of candidates for the Matura, the final school examination in 1929. On this occasion they kindly made me about six months older, in order to spare me from having to first obtain written permission from my parents.

*

My father, Abraham Stroumsa (see p.85), was a teacher of Hebrew, Ladino (precisely, Sephardic, the language of the Sephardic Jews) and Jewish history in the schools of the Jewish community. At the same time, he also taught at 'Alcheh', a private school, which at that time was directed by the brothers Isaak and Albert Alcheh. These two brothers were quite different not only physically, but also in their intellectual interests: Isaak was strong, large and an imposing figure, while Albert was delicate and not as vigorous, but possessed a certain elegance. Isaak instructed us in bookkeeping and introduced us to Judaism in the weekly Torah readings, while Albert taught the exact sciences.

The school had been founded by their father Jakob Alcheh as early as ca. 1880, and after the fire of 1917 it was moved to the rural residential area not far from the Aghia Triada, the Church of the Trinity. Admission to this school was especially valued by the Jewish middle class, which formed the dominant social stratum of the Jewish community.

At that time the Jewish population could be divided into roughly three groups: the children from the socially lowest strata attended the schools of the Alliance Israélite Universelle, where pupils learned Hebrew and French. Other children attended the schools of the Jewish community, where the language of instruction was first of all Hebrew, then more and more Greek and Hebrew. The well-to-do sent their children to the Alcheh School or even to schools abroad, such as, for example, the Mission Laique Française, the private religious school for boys, 'Saint Joseph', or the convent schools for girls. Foreign schools, such as the Italian, German or Romanian schools, were very fashionable.

My father, who had received his education in the Great Talmud-Torah School, an institution for the training of Jewish teachers, taught not only at the community schools, but also at the Alcheh School. In order to augment the family income, my father also taught the boys who were approaching their Bar-Mitzvah, the celebration of religious majority on the occasion of their thirteenth birthday, who came to him to learn the required passages from the Torah.

His sonorous voice and inexhaustible patience had made him, by far, the most beloved teacher among the best families of the city. Later, when I was an engineering student in Paris, he asked me to visit a few of his former pupils, who in the meantime had assumed important positions, as for example Nahmias, in Petrofrance, David Sciaky, as possessor of a welding machine factory, Yeni and others.

My mother (p.11), Doudoun, whose maiden name was Yoel, was the niece of a well-known gynecologist, Dr. Meir Yoel, and herself a highly talented milliner. Her atelier was located at home, in our family house at Number 13 Zaímiss Street, which at that time was situated in a rural district near the Pathé Cinéma, rather far from the city's shopping and industrial areas.

Mother had several pupils, often young girls who had just finished secondary school, they came from the Alcheh School or from the Mission Laique Française to learn the trade of seamstress, usually up until their marriage. The most important mainstay of the atelier was my mother's younger sister, my beloved aunt Estrea, who remained in our house until her marriage to Isaak Yahiel, in the year 1922. Isaak was an accountant at the well-known firm of 'Les Moulins Allatini'. They later became parents of two wonderful boys, Jacques and Guillaume.

It was more than just friendship that bound us to my aunt and uncle, even inspite of the fact that the atmosphere at the beginning of their marriage was poisoned by the mother-in-law's irascible personality. This was my uncle Isaak's mother, who seemed to come from another planet, for she was just plain jealous of our extended family because it had robbed her of her only son. Arguments were frequent, and occasionally they took on a very acrimonious character. There were alway arguments, as long as this mother-in-law was alive. After her death, life became more normal, but difficulties of another sort arose. Apparently, the shares of the Allatini Company changed hands and one day nearly all the Jewish employees were dismissed with thanks for their former services. My uncle lost his job and simultaneously his apartment, which was owned by the company. However, he quickly found another job, and he and his family moved into the second story of our house, paying us a modest rent.

My uncle Isaak died unexpectedly from a simple inflamed appendicitis, which was operated on too late. This was a catastrophe for the entire family, above all, of course, for my poor aunt, left a widow with two small children. My cousin Jacques consequently began to earn his living relatively early, but soon afterward the war in Albania intervened. Unfortunately, my memories of this period are quite vague.

*

What I do remember very well is a reunion with my cousin Jacques in Auschwitz. I discovered him in an isolated barracks. Everyone sent there had been selected for the gas chamber. Despite the restrictions, I managed to see him. The block was a prohibited area that no one was permitted to leave. Thus we could only wave to each other, with tears in our eyes. He suffered from an inflammation under one of his fingernails which had been neglected from the start and had become seriously infected. Jacques was chosen for execution as he lay in the infirmary.

Later, after our evacuation from Auschwitz, I was marched over to Mauthausen. It was the 25th of January, 1945, and very cold. A thick blanket of snow covered the camp's vast courtyard. After our shower there was a roll-call and a second roll-call. Finally the order came to move into the barracks. We were stiff from cold and more dead than alive. In this filthy building, where one could scarcely find a place to sit on the floor, I suddenly caught sight of my cousin, Guillaume Yahiel, poor Jacques' younger brother. He was alive, yes he was alive, but he was so wasted down to nothing that I couldn't hold back my tears. It cost him a great effort to reach and embrace me, for the barrack was full to overflowing. He was a very tall man, and that made him seem even more emaciated.

After a few days, fate separated us again. Much later I learned that he had been rescued and had returned to Salonica, where he enjoyed the best of care. Shortly thereafter he had the good fortune to receive a visa for the USA. To my great joy I was later able to visit him twice in San Antonio, Texas, where he lives in the midst of his loving family.

*

Our house in Salonica was three stories high and situated next to the new 'Yeni-Djami' mosque, which had been built by the Turks shortly before my birth. This mosque was an especially beautiful structure, and so after the liberation of the city in October 1912, the Greeks decided to preserve it as an historically valuable monument and set up an archaeological museum in it. I remember seeing the French Minister President Herriot there on his official visit in 1925. He had to visit it since he was also the president of the 'Mission Laique Française'.

I was the oldest of four children, two boys and two girls. My sister Julie was born in 1915, my brother Guy, 1918, and finally my sister Bella, the youngest, was born on 17 November 1923. Coincidentally, my daughter Annie first saw the light of day in Paris in 1950 on the very same date. We never had any family quarrels, and the fact that my father also tutored several pupils at home probably contributed to the fact that our home had a certain climate of seriousness and integrity. The children of Professor Stroumsa *had* to be models for the other pupils (see pp.10-12)!

One or two years before my Bar-Mitzvah, my mother decided that I ought to learn to play a musical instrument. We went to her cousin Yoel, who ran a large music shop. Everyone thought that I should begin by learning the mandolin. The cousin acquainted us with the appropriate professor, who taught at the 'Conservatoire Grecos'. Suddenly a new world was opened up for me.

Less than a year had passed when my teacher had to inform my father that there was nothing more that he could teach me, and advised him that I should exchange the mandolin for a violin. Thus I soon became the favorite pupil of Professor Livio Marchesini. I was an especially enthusiastic pupil and made very rapid progress. I was talented and had a good ear and an excellent musical memory. My violin lessons were scheduled twice each week on Mondays and Thursdays from five to six o'clock. I would not have missed those lessons for anything in the world.

I remember one particular incident I had at the Alcheh School which made quite a stir and is an example of my fervor. I must have done my assignment in bookkeeping too poorly to satisfy Isaak Alcheh, the director of the school, and a penalty was imposed at once. „This afternoon you will stay after class for two hours and copy the assignment twenty times!" Unfortunately it was a Monday. When the large clock in the laboratory where I was sitting out my punishment struck four o'clock, I was terrified. I grabbed the violin, which I had carefully concealed, raced out the door and ran to the streetcar, anxious to arrive on time for my lessons at the Conservatory.

As expected, the next morning I learned that my absence had been noticed. Isaak Alcheh, displaying no visible sign of excitement, requested that I step forward from the row of desks and asked why I had disappeared so suddenly the day before. I mustered all my courage and replied, „You have the right to punish me if you believe that I have earned a punishment. But - please not on Monday or Thursday, the days when I have my violin lessons! They are as important in my eyes as a physics or mathematics lesson!" I saw how Isaak Alcheh flushed with anger and heard him call to my father, „Avram, mira que tu hijo tiene cabessa eskenazi! - Abraham, your son really has the head of an Ashkenazi!" He wanted to indicate that I had a thick skull. Ashkenazi, the Jews of German or Eastern European origin, were known for having wills of iron. This incident was over, but thereafter whenever an occasion for administering punishment arose, the director would ask, with a twinkle in his eye, „What day is it today?"

All during my school days, Zionistic sentiment was flourishing. It wasn't without reason that the Jerusalem rabbis spoke of Salonica as the „little Israel of the diaspora," or even as the „Jerusalem of the Balkans." Jewish life there was extraordinarily vigorous. After the death of Theodor Herzl (1904), the Jews of Salonica became zealous champions of Zionism, but could only work secretly, for in the Ottoman Empire Zionism was forbidden until 1912.

In the meantime, several Zionist groups organized, the most important of which - Maccabi, Mizrachi (religious Zionists), the Association of Young Jews (A.Y.J.) - belonged to the international Zionist movement. Since the home of the Maccabi was located in the immediate vicinity of our house, and there was a wind group and an orchestra there directed by Isaak Zion (He later died in Auschwitz), I was happy to accept his invitation to play with the orchestra. I immediately received the position of first violinist, and my memories of this time have remained quite vivid.

There could be no Jewish celebration without the participation of the Maccabi, the wind group, or of the orchestra. Even during my military service I remained loyal to the orchestra, always as first violinist, and every Saturday evening we played in the officers mess.

For years, the upper stories of the Tour Blanche, the famous crusaders' tower, which even today dominates the sea promenade of Salonica (the Boulevard Nikis), was rented to youth groups. The Maccabi occupied almost an entire floor, and for several years our meetings took place in this tower. Each time I visit Salonica, seeing the Tour Blanche again moves me in a very special way. I have told my children of it so often that my youngest daughter, Florence, brought a precious gift back from a trip to Paris. At the bouquinistes on the banks of the Seine she had discovered a beautiful postcard which pictured the Tour Blanche in the period around 1917. I framed the card and hung it over my desk.

Besides the athletic and cultural associations in Salonica, there were numerous *Yeshiwót*, purely religious Jewish schools which maintained a low profile. Their pupils were indistinguishable from the pupils from other schools, even in their clothing. Therefore we others scarcely noticed that there were other institutions of Jewish culture and education that existed.

To be sure, the Jewish community played a very important role in Salonica, but it was dispersed throughout the different sections of the city, except for the northern district, where the really poor people lived close together. Thus, for example, Doctor Israel, the father of our friends Charles and Rachel, was known everywhere as the „Poverty Doctor," because he exclusively visited patients who lived in the northern parts of the city, Aghia Paraskevi, Regie Vardar, Baron de Hirsch, among others.

2. Studies in Paris and military service at home

After secondary school I decided to study engineering at the university level in France. This decision was influenced by Engineer Leitmer, my mathematics teacher. I cannot emphasize enough how much respect I felt for him, and he also liked me. He was a model not only for me, but also for all of my best friends: the brothers Jacques and Pepo Kohen, the brothers Saragossi, the brothers Viktor and David Nahmias; Ezra and Aaron Rousso; Isaak Toledano and many others who died in Auschwitz. Leitmer had studied at the engineering school, E.I.M., in Marseilles and possessed, above all, extraordi-nary pedagogical abilities as a mathematics teacher. In addition, he was my primary influence during my first year of studying in Marseilles.

That first year, when I was accepted by the E.I.M and simultaneously by the faculty for natural sciences (which at that time was located behind the Gare Saint-Charles), was a wonderful year for me in every respect. The next year I went to Paris, where all my comrades from Salonica studied (among them were Jacques and Pepo Cohen, brothers who remained my friends up until they died in Israel).

My stay in France was unforgetable. Thanks to the extraordinary generosity of the French authorities, a scholarship allowed me to complete my studies and lead an unpressured and pleasant student life. Sundays I usually attended the afternoon concerts and then went to the Prado or the Jardin des Plantes with a few comrades for ice cream on the Cannebière.

It was marvelous to be on my own in such a progressive city as Marseilles in 1930. I could take long excursions, because there were numerous streetcar lines to the surrounding villages, some more than an hour away. Occasionally I traveled on Sunday with my friend Poeti to one of these villages where we were invited to have lunch with his aunt.

There were however other activities which were less enjoyable. In all French higher educational institutions the custom existed of celebrating the *Père Cent*, a festivity which usually took place a hundred days before the completion of the school year. In the engineering schools each *Bizut* (new-comer) usually had a mentor who was a third year student. His task consisted in helping the newcomer in difficult situations and initiating him into the student community, but above all to stand by and assist him at large festivities.

The celebration began with a large meal in a well-known restaurant on the lower Cannebière. Afterwards, when we had rather more than satisfied our thirst, we lined up outside to relieve ourselves from a scenic overlook above the Vieux-Port. Then in the adjoining streets we divided up into small groups and began to sing bawdy songs.

All along these streets, which have ceased to exist, there were an abundance of bordellos, recognizable by the red lamps outside. A few had been reserved especially for us. Completely terrified, I clung to my mentor; for this was a world that was still entirely unknown to me.

When we reached the second story a swarm of young women pounced on us. A mattress lay in the middle of the large salon, and each lady sought out her customer. *Faire l'amour* - here one was supposed to perform before all eyes. Naturally one of these young ladies approached me with the aim of initiating me into the art of love making. I flushed crimson to the roots of my hair and owed my rescue only to my mentor, who took my place! No one could imagine that I was still a virgin.

I successfully completed my first year of studies, but decided to continue my studies in Paris, so that I could be together with my friends from Salonica, to whom I was greatly attached. If Marseilles had fascinated me from the very start, Paris was for me entirely different: I discovered the City of Lights!

After three years in Paris, having been awarded an electro-engineering diploma by the E.S.M.E., the *Ecole Spéciale de Mécanique et d'Electricité*, I decided to attend the University of Bordeaux for a further year in order to study radio-telegraphy. In 1935 I had the good fortune of also being admitted to the Conservatory of Bordeaux, directed at that time by Professor Gaston Poulet. I thus attended both the University and the Conservatory, where I was chosen for the orchestra class.

Why Gaston Poulet liked me so much I do not know. I only remember that in Paris, after the liberation in 1945, my attention was attracted by a poster bearing the words „Concerts Poulet," announcing a concert subscription in the Théâtre Sarah Bernhardt. I hurriedly bought a ticket and in the intermission I slipped behind the coulisse. What then occurred I can scarcely describe: The maestro recognized me from afar and immediately hurried toward me, just as I was attempting to reach him. He wrapped me in his arms and said softly, „How happy I am to know that you are alive!" There was no time to tell him that having been his student may have saved my life! Already he was being called to continue the concert. Tears in my eyes, I returned to my place.

*

At the end of 1935, after a very interesting technical practicum at Radio L.L. - at the time a very successful radio station owned by Lucien Levy - I resigned myself to returning home to my native city of Salonica, as I had promised my father.

After a scenic journey, by train from Paris to Marseilles, by ship to Piraeus, and then again by train, I arrived at last, in good health, in Salonica. Everyone was curious to learn whether I had a girlfriend, or even several, and why I had come home unmarried. Before my departure my father had made me promise on the *Mezuza** that I would return alone without any ties, as he had sent me to study and bring back a diploma, „When your time has come, you will marry one of our women in our presence and with our consent!" I wanted to keep this promise.

In fact, at that time I was still too immature to found my own household; I was young, had no position and still had to do my military service, which was the most urgent immediate task.

*

Consequently, I reported for duty with the 50th infantry regiment in Salonica and hoped that I would be accepted for the officers school in Rouf near Athens. However, an anti-Semite serving at the headquarters, a high ranking senior officer from Salonica, Lieutenant Colonel Nikolaidis, rejected me despite my two engineering diplomas. To be honest, I must of course add that the matter attracted a certain amount of notoriety, and thereafter all my Jewish comrades with university-level diplomas were admitted to the reserve officers school when they applied.

As for me, I came to terms with my situation. After a few months of basic training I was promoted to sergeant. At that time our captain, who held me dear, asked me to come to his office, „Listen, the Major, Commandant of the XIth infantry division, is seeking a soldier who can give him French lessons. I thought

---

* Literally „door post," the capsule on the right side of the frame of the entrance door to a Jewish dwelling with a small parchment roll and inscription from *Deuteronomy* 6, 4-9 and 11, 13-21 (fifth book of the *Torah*).

of you; for of all the people in our company, you are the only one who has studied in France and therefore the only one suitable for this task!"

A little later I was introduced to the Major, who exercised the functions of a general. I was greatly impressed by this man, who was very friendly and made every effort to please. He asked me to take a seat and thrust the morning newspaper *Progrès* under my nose so I could read aloud to him. I do not know how it happened, but at any rate I heard myself retort, „Sir, you are the pupil, You must read!" This remark amused him and he replied, „This young man, although small, is nevertheless 'oho'!" He began to read, and I corrected certain errors, above all in his pronunciation. At the end of the session he said, „I like you and would be pleased if you could come to my home everyday at six o'clock!"

Consequently I spent the time during my military service most pleasantly. Every Saturday evening I played in the orchestra of the garnison officers mess, where the officers spent a few hours together with their wives, dancing and listening to the music. Meanwhile, the General made progress with his French, and we were satisfied with each other. Later I had to reconcile myself to his transfer. When he went to the General Staff in Athens we were both very sad about the separation. Happily the remainder of my military service was devoted exclusively to music. My chief duties involved playing in the military orchestra.

After completing military service I began my professional life. I started in the Industrial Ministry, and then I worked in the Motor Division of the Agricultural Ministry, whose workshops were located in the north of Salonica. The experiences which I acquired at both these workplaces were very useful because I became acquainted with both the small and mid-sized industries of the city. I also worked on equipping tractors with diesel motors which were imported from Germany. My knowledge of German, acquired at the Goethe-Institute, enabled me to read the operating instructions in the original versions. I further perfected my German through additional evening courses.

3. German oppression and cruel deportation

On October 28, 1940, fully unexpectedly and with no declaration of war, Italy, which had already occupied Albania three years earlier, drove about sixty kilometers into Greek territory. Mussolini actually believed that he could occupy the large harbors of Greece unopposed. The famous „Ochi - No!" of General Metaxas struck like a bolt of lightning and quickly sobered him.

At this time, about 70,000 Jews were living in Salonica. About 1,000 had Italian and Spanish passports; all others were Greek citizens. Approximately 13,000 Jewish soldiers, among them 340 officers, bravely fought six months long in the Greek army. As the Germans took cognizance of the fact that the Italians had no success in advancing into Greece, they themselves undertook a massive assault, first from Yugoslavia, then through Thrace on the Bulgarian-Greek border.

Fortunately, I did not have to fight against the Germans. My regiment, the 50th I.R., was stationed in the rear front line in the mountainous area surrounding the city of Janina. For almost six long months we fought against the Italians and had already occupied about a third of the territory of Albania. Then in May 1941 we received by radio the order to lay down our weapons.

With the greatest respect I recall our Commander Major Mandouvalos, who called all the Jewish soldiers to him and gave the following address, „Greek soldiers of Jewish origin! We know that the Germans do not love us; however, we wish to do everything possible so that you will return home safely. Therefore we ask you to temporarily assume Greek names and forenames; we are going to give you identity cards with names you yourselves will choose!"

After the war was lost for the Greeks, we were demobilized. The army gave me a little donkey with which I could, without great difficulty, ride the 650 kilometers back to Salonica. About 100 kilometers before the Vardar river I received the good advice to sell the little donkey for a seat in a shared taxi which would bring us to our destination. I was then in great danger of being arrested by the Germans, to be put to work in forced labor gangs constructing new bridges over the river, since the Greek army had blown up all the old bridges. In order that I could pass through this area undetected, my countrymen disguised me as a woman. For the duration of the trip, I sat comfortably squeezed between two portly farm women on the back seat of the taxi. We were able to cross the bridge unhindered, and two hours later I was with my family, still heavily made up and dressed in women's clothes.

After my return from the army I was unemployed because, in the meantime, the technical facilities of the Agricultural Ministry had been bombed. My father, always generous in anything that concerned me, said, „If you think you could find something interesting at the university, I will enroll you!" I was accepted at the University of Salonica for the third year program in physics and mathematics.

*

The German occupation of Salonica lasted approximately three-and-a-half years, precisely from April 8, 1941, to October 30, 1944. As expected, the Jews above all were to suffer during the occupation. The persecutions can be divided into essentially three phases.

The first phase lasted from April 9, 1941, to July 11, 1942. I remember that upon my return from the army complete peace reigned in the city. Following a period of curfew, imposed after the German invasion, the inhabitants began to go out again, the streetcars resumed their regular traffic between the different quarters of the city, businesses opened and life resumed its normal course.

That seemed remarkable to me, after our heartfelt fear, seeing the German soldiers in our city. I found, however, that these soldiers were completely uninterested in the fate of the Jews; this seemed very reassuring, but did not fit with everything that we had previously heard.

It was during this time that I married - proof that we were not especially worried about the future. My wife, Nora Mordoh, belonged on her mother's side to the family of the Benrubi, who owned the most important shops for glassware, not only in Salonica, but in all Greece. On her father's side, Nora was descended from the equally important Mordoh family; the city administration of Salonica is housed, even today, in one of their villas.

I had met Nora even before the Albanian campaign of October 1940. She had sent packages to the front for me containing everything to help me bear the hardships of the winter and wrote very tender letters which gave me the strength to withstand the cold and the war. Upon my fortunate return, I told my parents about the aid of this young girl during the Albanian winter, and they agreed to our marriage. The ceremony took place in the Beit-Shaul Synagogue, the oldest and most beautiful synagogue of the city, which after the deportation of the Jews was blown up by the Germans.

We lived with my parents-in-law. They had a piano, which Nora liked to play, while I accompanied her on the violin. One morning, however, German police came and the piano was forcibly carted away, without our receiving as much as a receipt. Of course we had known that aggressive acts of this sort could increase, always at the expense of the Jews.

*

The second period of German occupation extended from July 11, 1942 to February 25, 1943. With the arrival at the beginning of February 1943 of the Chief Commissar for Reich Security, a henchman of Adolf Eichmann, plus two SS-Hauptsturmführer, Dieter Wisliceny and Alois Brunner, the systematic destruction of the Jews of Salonica began. Brunner lived safely for years under the pseudonym „Georg Fischer," and perhaps is still living, in Damascus.* Wisliceny was sentenced to death and executed in Czechoslovakia in 1948. In only three months time these two men had the entire Jewish population of Salonica deported.**

The „Jewish Laws" were thus drastically imposed on the Jewish population of Salonica: Confiscation of radio receivers, a ban on use of telephones, a prohibition against using public transport vehicles such as trams, busses, etc., a curfew from six o'clock in the evening to six o'clock in the morning and mandatory wearing of the yellow star.

The Greek press informed us that on July 11, 1942, at 9 o'clock in the morning all Jewish men from 16 to 45 years would have to assemble on Liberty Square. More than 9,000 men, among them also my brother and I, obeyed this order. I heard cries and the crack of whips. Young men were compelled to perform embarrassing and humiliating exercises, e.g., hopping like frogs while onlookers leaned out of windows to gape at this spectacle. Several men fainted, victims of torture and the harsh sun. The Germans splashed buckets of cold water over them to revive them for further torture.

We had to stay at this square until about two o'clock in the afternoon, and only thanks to the intercession of a Belgian Red Cross representative were we permitted to return home. He threatened the presiding German officers that he

---

* In December 1992 there was a report that Brunner had died in Syria; other reports, to the contrary, held that he was residing in Egypt. On May 18, 1995, the *International Herald Tribune* reported that „he may have left his hideout in Damascus and quietly slipped away to Latin America." Apparently, Brunner has become an embarrassment to Syria. Reportedly in Argentina, he is „the most senior Nazi thought to still be at large. He would be 83 if he is alive." Interviewed by the German magazine *Bunte* in 1985, Brunner said that „he was not sorry for what he had done and described the Jews as garbage who deserved to die." He „directed the deportation of 47,000 Jews from Vienna and 44,000 Greek Jews from Thessaloniki." ERW.
** Cf. R. Hilberg, *Die Vernichtung der europäischen Juden 1933-1945*, Vol. 2, Frankfurt 1990, p. 737.

would report on what was happening to General Field Marshal Wilhelm List, Chief of the German Wehrmacht in the South-East. We were allowed to leave the square only under the condition that on July 13 we would again assemble at the same time.

My brother Guy and I resolved not to obey this second order. That was a fortunate decision, for on that day a large number of Jews were drafted for forced labor in climatically unhealthy areas of Greece. Many of them fell victim to inadequate hygiene and lack of care and died during this work. The community was forced to pay the fabulous sum of a billion Drachmas to replace the Jews with other special workers.

We had the impression that the Germans aimed both to terrorize the Jewish population by drafting the men for forced labor and to destroy the Jewish community by extorting all its available funds. But we could absolutely not conceive that we were experiencing only the prelude to something much more terrible.

Finally, the famous historical cemetery of Salonica, which dated back to the fifteenth century, was desecrated and destroyed.

*

The Head Rabbi of Salonica, Dr. Zvi Koretz, still poses a question of conscience for us: Should we regard him as a traitor to the Jewish community of Salonica or not? Such a difficult question must not remain unexamined. The problem is dealt with in detail by a text, *In memoriam*, by Michael Molho and Joseph Néhama; here I will limit myself to merely a few comments (Cf. M. Molho (ed.), In memoriam, Essen 1981, see pp.103-104).

Of Polish origin, Koretz studied philosophy at the University of Vienna, where he also acquired his doctorate, as well as a perfect command of the German language. After settling in Salonica, he quickly learned Greek and seemed to be the right man to represent the Jews before the German authorities. However, too strongly convinced of his own abilities, he soon became an impatient egoist who would accept advice from no one.

On May 17, 1941, while on a business trip to Athens, he was taken into custody by the Gestapo and deported to Vienna, where he was interned for about eight months, probably in a concentration camp. No one knows under what circumstances and for what price he was freed. Returning to Salonica, he resumed his office as Chief Rabbi.

Meanwhile the German authorities quickly learned that President Saby Saltiel, whom they had installed, was not the right man for the hard task they had given him, even less so because he spoke not a word of German. Therefore, the deputy

Gestapo director, Dr. Kalmes, recommended Dr. Koretz for his position, even against the will of the Community Council. This position attracted Dr. Koretz, as it promised him almost dictatorial full powers, and so he accepted. From December 11, 1942, on he thus simultaneously exercised the functions of Chief Rabbi and President of the Jewish community of Salonica.

After having been imprisoned, it seems hardly credible that Dr. Koretz, as an intelligent person, could not see that the Germans wanted only to use him to deceive the Jewish community of Salonica. Nevertheless, he held a speech before the Community Council, in the course of which he pointed out that in Germany there was no lack of either white bread or butter, „Just look at me," he said, „do I look undernourished after my return from imprisonment in Vienna?"

On the evening of March 14, 1943, the evening before the first transport, at the bidding of the *Sicherheitsdienst*, Dr. Koretz called a meeting in the Baron de Hirsch Synagogue for the purpose of instructing the ghetto's residents that on the next day they would be transported to Cracow. Was he really unaware at this point in time that the destruction of the Polish Jews had already begun?

We will never determine the answer to this profoundly disturbing question. Still, it can hardly be assumed that Koretz had heard nothing at all. But did he also know of the existence of gas chambers and crematoria? We cannot say. We can, at any rate, suspect that he, as an educated and intelligent person, had read *Mein Kampf.* Was he not fully aware that the Germans would physically exterminate the Jews of Salonica after they had already robbed them of all they possessed?

To conclude this chapter: The Chief Rabbi and his family, along with other notables of the community, were brought to Bergen-Belsen under fairly tolerable circumstances. Dr. Zvi Koretz succumbed to illness even before the end of the war. Dr. Nathan Eck, first Director of Yad Vashém, published a major article in the *Yad Vashém Bulletin* (No. 17, December 1965, pp. 9) in which he attempts to defend the case of Chief Rabbi Koretz; this appears, however, to be hardly possible.[*]

But on the other hand, one should pay homage to Chief Rabbi Barzilay of Athens, who came from Salonica, for under the eyes of the Germans he summoned up the courage to give the Jewish population, assembled in the Synagogue on Melidonis Street, the advice, „*Fouyendovos todos*! - Everyone flee!" He took his own advice and with his wife and daughter went underground, where they held out until the liberation, often under very difficult circumstances. But he came back alive, along with everyone who took his advice.

---

[*] Cf. E. Kolb, *Bergen-Belsen 1943-1945*, Göttingen 1985, pp. 24; R. Hilberg 1990, pp. 737.

The third period of German occupation extended from February till August 1943. During this period, the Baron de Hirsch Ghetto was founded, Jewish capital was confiscated, the municipal archive was destroyed by a fire and, finally, the Jews were deported, with their „official destination" the city of Cracow.

The Baron de Hirsch Ghetto was set up in a Jewish quarter, which had been established by Baron de Hirsch to house people made homeless by the great fire of 1917, and was located across from the Central Railroad Station. About 3,000 people lived there. The Germans surrounded this area with high wooden fences on all sides and made three exits, one of which led to the railroad tracks.

As an engineer, I worked voluntarily for the Jewish community, helped to transfer the bones from the former Jewish cemetery, worked on the fencing off of the ghetto and, in addition, had the assignment of fitting out the interior of a building for the German Secret Service. On this occasion I got to know more of Wisliceny and Brunner, the Gestapo officers in charge of the deportations and since I understood a little German, I also overheard fragments of their conversations.

When they arrived we believed that these two hangmen had come to impose the Nuremberg Laws. One day, when the Baron de Hirsch Ghetto was ready and I was installing an electrical cable, I overheard a telephone conversation between Wisliceny, who was standing not far from me, and Brunner, who was obviously at the Gestapo office, „I think that the Jewish deportations could begin in a week!" This statement struck me like a bomb. Thus it was not simply a matter of setting up a ghetto; to the contrary, it was from the start a deportation plan. This term still meant nothing to us. Chief Rabbi Koretz, however, surely knew what was being plotted, but the members of our Community Council could never have conceived of such a thing.

On that particular day, I quickly completed my work and went home. On the way I met a member of the Community Council and told him what I had just heard, „Look out for yourself, my friend! We must avoid everything which could create panic among the population. If you say that to anyone, I will give your name to Chief Rabbi Koretz, and you will be in danger of being informed on to the Gestapo!" I listened to him and kept silent.

On Sunday, March 14, 1943, the *Sicherheitsdienst* (Security Service) ordered the Chief Rabbi and President, Dr. Zvi Koretz, to assemble all the Jews in the ghetto at the synagogue located there so that he could inform them about their impending deportation to Cracow. At 11 o'clock in the morning all the Jews who had been herded into the ghetto waited to hear what was happening. Koretz informed them that the great Jewish community of Cracow would welcome them as brothers: „Each of you will find a satisfying job in accord with his abilities and knowledge and appropriate to his professional experience!"

All those present broke out in tears. It was heartbreaking to realize that all hope was gone, „Heaven is deaf to all our prayers," writes the Community Rabbi Michael Molho in his text, *In memoriam*. Souls filled with fear of death, they prepared for their departure in the direction of Cracow. Everyone received a check for 600 Zlotys, whose exchange value in Drachmas was paid and noted down by the Gestapo. The farce thus continued up until the last moment.

After the departure of the people living in the ghetto the next morning, it was quickly filled with the Jewish residents of the nearby Aghia Paraskevi quarter. Ten thousand people were suddenly and brutally driven together in the narrow confines of the ghetto, which had been planned for at most 3,000 persons. The deportations continued in contingents of 3,000 every second or third day. We, who lived on the other side of the city, had reconciled ourselves to the idea that our turn would also come and that we were destined to live together with our brothers and sisters in Poland.

*

At the time of our deportation, my wife Nora, who was barely twenty years old, was in the eighth month of pregnancy. We had not the slightest foreboding of what lay ahead of us. Just a short time before, I had taken her to our neighbor and friend, the renowned gynecologist Dr. Luigi Modiano. After he thoroughly examined my wife, he turned to me and said, „Jacques, you have no cause to be worried! Nora's pregnancy is taking a completely normal course. My colleague in Cracow will attend the delivery just as I would have done it myself!" And so we went about our daily lives as though nothing out of the ordinary was going to happen. Thousands of Jews were sent to the ghetto and deported in the transports, but we made no effort to flee, go into hiding or otherwise escape from our fate.

The dates of the transports are precisely recorded: departure times, total number of deportees, KZ numbers of the men, number of men, KZ numbers of the women, number of women, total number of those who were immediately killed (see p.91).

My family and I were assigned to the sixteenth transport, which consisted at its departure of 2,500 persons. Numbers were assigned to 568 men and 247 women, i.e., a total of 815 persons. The other 1,685 persons were murdered immediately upon their arrival.

The deportation occurred with an indescribable cruelty. We were herded into cattle cars, approximately 80 persons per wagon - men, women, the elderly, the sick, the children. In every wagon there was a single bucket of drinking water. Apart from what each family was allowed to take with them, raisins, dried figs, etc., there was no food. In lieu of toilets the railroad administration had provided a tub for each wagon which was completely inadequate to serve the bodily needs of so many people. It was so crowded that people could barely sit down and mostly had to stand. The inadequate ventilation consisted of air admitted through two small loopholes, covered by wire mesh.

From time to time the externally locked wagon doors were opened in order to empty the tubs and provide us with drinking water. At one of these stops, probably at a small train station in the vicinity of Vienna, the doors were suddenly thrown open. On the platform appeared SS-Führer Brunner, who knew me from the Baron de Hirsch Ghetto. He walked along beside the train and seemed to be searching for a familiar face. When he saw me, he made a sign that, along with another young man, I should climb down. We thus both left the wagon, and he signaled for us to follow him.

Arriving at his compartment in a normal railroad wagon, he ordered us to carry a heavy wooden chest to the chief entrance of the station and after that a second chest, which was just a heavy as the first. Then he sent us back to our wagon and soon after that the train began to move again. What could have been in the chests? Perhaps gold and jewels stolen from our countrymen in Salonica? Recently the Investigatory Commission of a Frankfurt court came to Jerusalem to confirm this suspicion.

The train started again, and its tempo seemed to accelerate so we would not arrive too late at the appointed destination! By far, the most significant share of us were to face the 'final solution'!

4. Arrival, prisoner and violinist in Auschwitz

As far as I can remember, our transport, which had left Salonica one beautiful spring morning on the 30th of April, 1943, arrived in Auschwitz-Birkenau toward four or five o'clock in the morning on the 8th of May, 1943.* As we de-

---

* May 8, 1943: „With a transport of the RSHA from Greece 2,500 Jewish men, women and children arrive from the ghetto in Saloniki. After selection 568 men and 247 women and children are admitted as prisoners into the camp. They receive the numbers 120,650 to 121,217 and 44,380 to 44,626. The remaining 1,685 people are killed in the gas chambers." (D. Czech, *Kalendarium der Ereignisse im Konzentrationslager Auschwitz-Birkenau 1939-1945*, Reinbek and Frankfurt 1989, p. 490).

scended from the train, the harsh beam of a spotlight, the whips cracking, the shrill orders of the SS had the desired effect. The doors were thrown open, a horde of young men in blue-white striped prisoners' garb and armed with clubs swarmed around us like savages. They cried, „Out, everyone out, quick!" The air was rather chilly, almost cold. Blinded, deafened, numb, we were absolutely unable to understand exactly what they wanted of us. Confused and frightened, we climbed out quickly, leaving behind our personal possessions.

My brother Guy helped my parents and our sisters, Julie and Bella, out of the wagon. I held onto my eight-months-pregnant wife, Nora, with one hand and my violin with the other. Vicious blows compelled me to let go of both. First I entrusted Nora to her mother's care, and then I ran to my father to help and protect him. But then, what help could I give?

Deafened by the shouting, surprised by the early-morning cold of dawn, blinded by the spotlight beam, suddenly for the first time we were separated from our wives. I still vividly remember that, stumbling over the tracks, we received the order to divide up into two groups, young and old - and how I embraced my father once more, not knowing that I would never do so again.

I remember how I helped him to cross the tracks and how, in the moment that the SS separated us, I had barely time to kiss his right hand, as if wanting to receive his paternal blessing for the last time. I never saw him again. The young people had already been sent to the left side, while the elderly marched to the right. Covered trucks bearing the symbol of the Red Cross were parked at the end of the platform. For an instant we actually believed that the wagons were intended for the transport of the elderly men and women, while we younger persons were to march on foot. But we quickly realized that this was only a gesture of sadism. They had thought of every single mean, demonic trick (see pp. 94-95).

*

Soon we were subjected to interrogation by the SS. They drove us into a line with clubs so that we could march, one by one, past an SS officer seated behind a desk. My brother was behind me. We dared not speak, for already the questioning had begun: age, profession, languages, etc. One or two hours later we marched five abreast into the camp, after we had, without noticing it, been selected. We had been assigned to the group of workers between fifteen and fifty years of age.

We were then sent to a barrack where I suddenly caught sight of Dr. Morris Samuelidis, a friend from Salonica. He had arrived two or three transports earlier and was already working as a camp physician. Unobtrusively, Dr. Samuelidis took me aside and attempted to explain in a few words that we were in a KZ (abbr. for 'Konzentrationslager' - concentration camp) and what was to happen, or had already happened, to my parents, my poor wife Nora and my whole family.

Although I was completely beside myself and stood there, my eyes opened wide in horror, Morris continued without hesitating with the terrible description of what happened here in Birkenau, „By now," he said, „your wife, your parents and her parents have already been gassed, and soon they will be burned in the ovens of the crematorium. The young people brought to the camp have a chance, a small chance to survive, but only provided that they never become ill. They must work until the end of the war in their special areas..." - I had the impression that my friend had become insane, that he was raving!

For me the shock was doubly hard, because my Greek-Orthodox friends in Salonica had attempted several times to persuade me to join the Greek Liberation Army, E.A.M./A.G.M. But I had not wanted to follow their advice, simply for the reason that I did not want to abandon my wife and my parents, to whom I was so greatly attached. I had the feeling that I was their only support and thought that my engineering diploma would help them to survive, even in Poland.

Although bitterly disillusioned by the confidential conversation with Dr. Samuelidis, I nevertheless did not reproach myself for not actively resisting the deportation. My brother Guy, in the meantime, needed only to look at my horrified face, drained of all color, in order to guess the facts our countryman had whispered to me. Suddenly an SS-man appeared in the barrack and deathly silence ensued, preventing me from passing on the details of our private conversation.

*

Then we were made into real Birkenau prisoners. First, the prisoners' number was tattooed onto the left forearm. I received number 121097. After that we went to the barber; our hair was shaved off, not only on our heads, but over our entire bodies. Then we all had to shower, boiling hot - ice cold! Immediately after that we were made to put on our new blue-white striped prison uniforms with the prisoner's number on the left breast side with an inverted red triangle. Jews wore a superimposed yellow triangle, which created a six-pointed star. Later we learned that prisoners with a rose colored triangle were homosexuals.

A black triangle meant „asocial," a green triangle, „criminal."[*] The bearers of the green triangles were mostly Germans who had been hauled out of prisons and, as „block seniors," were responsible for their blocks. That meant they could decide over the life and death of the prisoners who were housed in their blocks (see p.92).

Thus we were now integrated into the life of the camp. All we lacked were the eating utensils, the „Miske," which was a container for a ladle of soup, tea or coffee, and a spoon. The soup was a disgusting brew containing beets, and the morning coffee or tea, a repulsive concoction that had the sole virtue of being warm. We very quickly learned to be on guard lest anything be stolen. For theft - called „organizing" - was a widespread practice in the camp. Of course we could not think of complaining. Losing our eating utensils was like a death sentence, for without them, how could we receive and consume the hot soup, coffee or tea?

After the unavoidable roll-call, which took place evenings in every sort of weather outside in front of the block, and often lasted for hours, we went inside the barracks where so-called beds and blankets were assigned to us. Our beds were bare wooden frames stacked three high, and three persons slept on each level. Once we were assigned to our beds, the block senior ordered us to the entrance of the block, where we had to assemble around him. Just catching the block senior's eye was terrifying, and soon we were overwhelmed by fear. This person, built like Hercules, always carried a club, and the green triangle on his breast constantly reminded us that we were dealing with a criminal. The word got around quickly that he was a former bank robber sentenced to a severe punishment whom the Nazis had hauled out of prison to take over the leadership of a block.

*

When we were all assembled around him, he asked, „Are there any prisoners here who play a musical instrument?" This question, posed by such a brutish person, was truly astonishing. After everything which we had experienced since our arrival, we should also be able to play an instrument! No one responded. But my comrades, who knew me from Salonica, instinctively turned to me, because they thought I should say that I played the violin, „*Puede ser es bueno para todos*!"- Maybe that would be good for us all?!

---

[*] Cf. D. Czech, *Kalendarium der Ereignisse im Konzentrationslager Auschwitz-Birkenau 1939-1945*, Reinbek and Frankfurt 1989, p. 113.

I gave in to comradely pressure, stepped forward and said in German, „I play the violin, but that is not my profession; when I was admitted to the camp I indicated that I am an electro-engineer!" Then I heard him say, „The fact that you did not reply to my question immediately, although you are in fact a violinist, is the purest sabotage, and you could have gotten twenty-five lashes on your butt! But because you say that you are only an amateur, five lashes will be enough! First, though, I would like to hear you play!" - „My instrument was taken away as we climbed out of the wagon this morning!" - „That doesn't matter, I will find a violin for you at once!"

And in fact - a few minutes later the „*Stubendienst*" (menial), that is the block senior's assistant, handed me a violin and a bow. Naively I asked, „What would you like to hear, Sir? Mozart, Beethoven, Haydn? A violin concerto or rather a sonata?" After I had tuned the instrument, I began to play. I remember having played uninterruptedly for about twenty minutes. Everyone was very touched, everyone recalled his free life in Salonica. This music seemed under the circumstances completely unreal. The block senior motioned for me to stop, came to me and remarked, „You play very well! And I know what I am talking about, for I am a pianist. Besides that, you are an engineer and speak good German!" He placed his hand on my shoulder and said, „I hope that you will not die on us here!" - A shudder ran through my limbs. - „We will skip the punishment, for you will be brought right away to the audition in the conservatory."

I followed the 'Stubendienst' to a barrack which served as Conservatory. Inside, prisoners had to audition one after the other. As my turn came, a large, gaunt prisoner stood before me, apparently the director of the orchestra. To my relief I immediately noticed an 'F' on the red triangle fastened to his uniform, and it occurred to me that he came from France, a glimmer of hope for me. „Are you a Frenchman, Sir?" I asked, pleased with this discovery. He barked at me, „Here there is no more 'Sir', here one person is as much a piece of filth as the next!" - „Unfortunately, which does not, however, change the fact that you are a Frenchman, and that gives me great pleasure!"

For his part he now looked at the letters on my red triangle and commented, „Aha, you arrived this morning on the transport from Salonica! Where did you receive violin lessons?" - As though one couldn't learn to play the violin in Salonica! A bit offended I replied, „First six years in Salonica, then in France: in Marseilles at the 'Lycée Musical', three years in Paris and above all at the Conservatory in Bordeaux, where I was the pupil of the great maestro Gaston Poulet!"

The last claim was not so accurate, for at the time when Gaston Poulet was Director of the Conservatory and the „Grand Théâtre de Bordeaux," he instructed only the violinists of the master class, who had already won their first prizes. At the same time, to be sure, he was also director of the Conservatory's student orchestra, in which I played. Anyway, I was taken on without audition as the first violinist in the orchestra of Auschwitz-Birkenau. My new chief also asked me, „Do you remember a café in Bordeaux where one could hear good classical music?" - „The Café du Commerce on the Allées de Tourny!" - „You see, I was the first violin there!" - So it happened that for a month I played as solo violinist in the camp orchestra."[*]

Once all the prisoners had left the camp, marching in step to the sounds of the orchestra, we returned to our barrack, and everyone could play what he wanted. We did not lack for scores. Since people from all parts of Europe had been driven together there, we found a very extensive musical literature, not including Jewish composers like Mendelssohn and others who were of course forbidden.

What did we musicians have to do? We stood in the cold at the morning roll-call for one or two hours or longer our teeth chattering when it drizzled. Every detachment prepared itself for work. We, the musicians of the orchestra, had to go to our Conservatory Barrack, fetch our instruments, quickly take our position on the balustrade before the main entrance of the camp and get ready. At the expected whistle, the orchestra, directed by our chief, began to play, while the slave laborers marched past, and at the command „Caps off!", each prisoner tore his cap from his head.

Woe to him who did not march in step! They were in rows of five, „pro-pince" in Polish, and in a monotone voice the person responsible counted before the entrance door, „One, two, three, four, five ... !" He counted thus to twenty - that meant a hundred prisoners, then he began again from the start. And we in the orchestra had to play on without interruption. That could last two hours or more, regardless of whether it was cold or raining. This machinery, once set in motion, could only stop at command, after all the carefully counted prisoners had left the camp.

Every block, including the Conservatory, was under the supervision of an SS-man. On the very first day, as we began our rehearsals, an SS supervisor suddenly appeared at the door. The shocked director motioned for us to stop and salute. But the SS-man screamed at us, „Keep on! Play on!" Slowly he came toward us and listened to our music. As he passed me, he noticed that I wanted to stop. Again he cried, „Keep on!" Therefore I played on and sensed how he stood next

---

[*] Cf. H. Langbein, *Menschen in Auschwitz*, Vienna 1972, pp. 150.

to me and guardedly slipped a cigarette into my left jacket pocket. Immediately after that he disappeared. Everything happened very quickly, and no one noticed anything.

*

At noon, as we ate our soup, I sat near my friend Dr. Maurice Algava. Crouching on the ground we attempted to absorb every weak sunbeam and warm ourselves a bit. When we had almost finished eating our soup, Maurice whispered to me, „Do you know, Jacob, that I brought a thousand cigarettes from Salonica and now not a single one is left?" At that time I hardly ever smoked, while Maurice liked to puff a few everyday. I remembered the scene from that morning and pulled out of my pocket a beautiful cigarette which I presented to my friend. He took it quickly with a glance at the brand, „That is definitely a German cigarette!" Maurice looked shocked. „Tell me, did you kill someone? How did this cigarette get into your pocket?" I told him the story of the Conservatory, and he could barely believe his ears. „Listen, Jacob, if your SS-man comes back again tomorrow, play whatever you have to, a concerto by Mozart or a Beethoven sonata, - the main thing is that you get a cigarette!" The astonishing thing was that the SS-man often came back. Each time he slipped me a cigarette which I guarded like a treasure for Maurice.

Later, when I worked in the planning office of the „Weichsel-Union Metal Works,"[*] it was my boss, Chief Engineer Bosch, who would empty his pipe of fresh tobacco into an ashtray and ask me to clean it. I exchanged this tobacco for soap, margarine or salami. My friend Maurice remained in Birkenau while I was transferred to Auschwitz; happily, after the liberation he returned safely to Paris, where we were able to renew our friendship which still continues today, despite the great distance. Again and again he has reminded me of the famous cigarettes of Birkenau and still maintains, „You couldn't give me a present which could beat the cigarettes you gave me then!"

---

[*] September 7, 1943: „The Friedrich Krupp AG is informed that the Weichsel-Union Metal Works, which possesses a fuse factory in Zaporoz'e, must be evacuated. Within ten to twelve days the machines and production facilities are to be transported to Auschwitz. [Zaporoz'e - a city in the Ukrainian Soviet Republic. On the 22th of August, 1943, Red Army tanks advanced to the Dnepr river below Kiev.] The following solutions are suggested for the Krupp Works: 1. take over the production of the Weichsel-Union Metal Works, 2. transfer production to the Weichsel-Union Metal Works, 3. form a combine." (D. Czech, *Kalendarium der Ereignisse im Konzentrationslager Auschwitz-Birkenau 1939-1945*, Reinbek and Frankfurt 1989, p. 600).

On Sundays we wanted to contribute the little that we could to encouraging our ill comrades. A few of us played in the „infirmary," the camp hospital. We had practiced a selection of pieces because we knew that some of the patients loved classical music.

*

Thirty-six years later I had an experience which showed the deep impression our music had made on some comrades whom we entertained Sundays in the hospital. In 1979 I earned a Doctorate in the Faculty of Architecture at the 'Technion', the Technical University of Haifa. My doctoral advisor, Professor Daniel Schefer, and I had the custom of working uninterruptedly, often forgetting to eat. Sometimes he would suddenly say, „Jacques, take a break, we will go and eat a sandwich and drink a good cup of coffee!" I could not have wished for anything better. After a brief stroll through the park we came out through a side exit on Herzl Street, and directly across from us there was a cafeteria where I had never been.

As soon as we entered, Schefer ordered and asked me in a loud voice, „And you, Jacques, what would you like?" At this moment something extraordinary happened. The manager of the cafeteria turned around, looked at me, hesitated a second, and then cried out, „Jacques, it is really you! Jacques Stroumsa, the violinist from Auschwitz who came to us Sundays in the hospital to play Mozart!" - The cafe was very small, with room for only a few customers, most of whom were professors from the „Technion." Upon hearing this cry of joy, everyone turned around. But aside from my professor, who knew of my KZ past, no one understood what was happening. The cafe's owner, Angelo Rajewski, was of Polish origin. He wept as though his long lost son had returned. Then his wife Rosa, who was likewise a survivor of the death camp, also came and embraced me, although she didn't know me at all.

Of course, I could not remember Angelo, but for him I was the violinist from Auschwitz, a man who had helped him spiritually to survive the worst hours in the infirmary by playing Mozart's A-major concerto. Only then did I learn how much Angelo loved music. After the liberation in May 1945 he and his wife Rosa emigrated to Brazil. When their two grown children moved to Israel, Angelo and Rosa followed them.

The little episode in the cafeteria quickly made the rounds in the 'Technion', and during the next few days I was asked again and again to recount my experiences in the orchestra of Auschwitz-Birkenau.

How did it happen that I left the orchestra? We all knew that the stay in Birkenau, the so-called Quarantine, was only of limited duration. One evening, exactly thirty days after our arrival in the camp, in the middle of distributing the coffee, the order rang out, „Achtung!" The „Stubendienst" began to call out numbers, and every prisoner who heard his number had to get ready at once. After a few minutes it was clear to us that there would be a transport of technicians, for besides me, other comrades with technical training were summoned. Now everyone who had identified himself as an electrician, painter or mechanic had to get ready as fast as possible to move out.

Thus a terrible question of conscience arose for me. My brother, Guy, the only family member who was still with me, had not reported himself as a technician and thus would have to remain in Birkenau. Bewildered, he came to me and asked, „What do you think, Jacques, should I claim at the last minute that I am a technician, electrician or mechanic so that I can stay with you?" We were both afraid of making a false declaration, because that could likewise have serious consequences. Therefore we said nothing, and a few minutes later we had to part forever after a last long embrace.

There was to be no reunion for us. No one among the few survivors could ever report to me even a hint concerning his further fate or death. He was a sturdy young man, but through hardship, privation and blows he was already very haggard. In memory of my father, Abraham, who was murdered on the very first day in Auschwitz-Birkenau, and my brother, we named our son, who was born in Paris on July 27, 1948, Albert-Guy.

5. Engineer at the Weichsel-Union Metal Works

On that the same evening we were brought to Auschwitz, which is about five kilometers from Birkenau. We were assigned to a block and threw ourselves on our straw sacks, almost out of our minds with grief. The only family member who was left to me in Birkenau, Guy, my dear brother, had now been taken from me. I sobbed in anger, because I could do nothing more for him.

On the next morning we thought that we would be assigned to technical detachments, each according to his training or his abilities. Imagine our great disappointment as we were lined up in rows and assigned to gardening inside the camp and ordered to keep the lawns in shape and lay out flower beds.

Auschwitz was occasionally visited by foreign delegations, prominent figures from the party or the Gestapo. The camp commanders wanted to make a good impression and show them that the prisoners, who worked as slaves during the day, returned evenings to a sort of golden cage in which, amid trees and flowers, everything would radiate a sense of order and tidiness. We were supposed to forget the kilometers of barbed-wire fences, surrounding us on all sides, the guard towers, the perpetually armed SS-men, their finger on the trigger, ready to shoot anyone who dared to approach them.

So already after a few days we had no illusions that we could work as qualified technicians. We had to dig, shove the spades deep into the hard earth and prepare the ground for planting flower beds. The beautiful grounds only served to painfully remind us of our own hopelessness and despair.

*

One evening I felt a piercing pain in the right lower side of my abdomen. I complained about this to my friend Leo Kohen (I was reunited with Leo in Salonica in April 1986) who was experiencing the same symptoms. We resolved to report to the doctor on the next day, in the naive hope of receiving a few days rest, which we called the „Blockschonung" (block convalescence). To our horror, the SS doctor diagnosed a ruptured hernia and dictated to his clerk, „Operation!"

Instead of a few days of rest they brought us to the infirmary, that is, the hospital. The surgeon, a former professor at the University Clinic in Warsaw and a political prisoner, decided after a brief examination to operate the next day. We did everything to make our comrades aware and also commended our souls to God. We had a terrible fear. Would they operate with or without anesthesia? How would they care for us? Who would hear our screams? I believe that we hardly closed an eye that night.

The next morning the medical orderly came very early in order to bring us for the necessary preparations, and soon after that I was brought into the operating room. The surgeon came to me and said very kindly, „You need have no fear, sit down here, I will give you a local anesthetic!" He took a long needle, placed it against my spinal column and injected a fluid into me which took effect immediately. The entire lower half of my body became numb. Then I was laid down, arms and legs strapped tight. I heard the clicking of the instruments, saw everything in the mirror of the lighting installation, but I felt no pain at all. Everything seemed to proceed normally.

It was impossible to understand the mentalities of our executioners. On the one hand, they beat people to death, murdered them in the most ingenious ways and, arbitrarily and on the flimsiest of pretexts, sent them to the gas chambers, even for a minor inflammation under a fingernail. On the other hand, there was an orchestra, a hospital with a proper operating room, local anesthetics to prevent pain, and everything, just so that after an operated rupture one could be back on one's feet as fast as possible, in order to go on doing endless slave labor. It was incomprehensible.

I was still occupied with my thoughts when suddenly the door opened, an SS-man entered and roared, „Warm here, much too warm!" He took off his belt, on which an oversized pistol hung, and threw it across my knees. „Now I'm in for it," I thought to myself, „he will kill me!" The SS-man went over to the window, threw it open wide and roared again, „No air! Here there is just no air!" No one dared contradict him. The operation had gone well, but the fresh air did its work. I caught a severe bronchitis which came within a hair's breadth of killing me.

A few days after that, as I lay on my back flushed with fever, a male nurse warned me, „A selection is going to be made now!" That meant that they picked out the „incurably" ill to send to the gas chambers. „Now you play dead! Under no circumstances do you move!" - No sooner said than done; he covered me from head to toe with a white sheet. A little later the selection commission passed by me, and I heard the nurse say, „This one is already dead!" After that the commission moved on to continue its macabre work.

*

A few weeks later and almost well, I was called to the block where the members of the technical detachment slept. The next day, after the endless roll-call, we marched to the Weichsel-Union Metal Works.* In my naivety I still supposed that they planned engineering work for me, but I was soon disillusioned. When the Capo saw that I did not really know where I should turn, he gave me a kick with the words, „You lazy pig, help me shove the wagon!" And so I found myself assigned to a group in which the large, burly Russian prisoners of war shoved wagons into the interior of the Works. That meant unloading machine parts which were afterwards assembled piece by piece.

---

* September 20, 1943: „The Weichsel-Union Metal Works, evacuated from Zaporoz'e, puts 137 prisoner technicians of the KL Auschwitz to work, presumably for the unloading of the transported machines and production facilities. On the following day it also makes use of an additional 200 prisoner helpers and 21 female prisoners. - In the Works of the Weichsel-Union Metal Works, during the last days of September, over 230 prisoner-technicians and 15 female prisoners are employed. The male prisoners are employed in assembling machines and facilities, the females are assigned cleaning and servicing tasks." (D. Czech, *Kalendarium der Ereignisse im Konzentrationslager Auschwitz-Birkenau 1939-1945*, Reinbek and Frankfurt 1989, p. 610).

After a few hours of this exhausting labor, which seemed endless, I was totally drained of strength. Then I asked one of my comrades whether he could point out the director of the Works. He pointed to the man at a distance, a large chap in an SS uniform, surrounded by a few of his henchmen, who seemed to obey him automatically. Without thinking what I was doing, I left my Russians and went directly to this man. Later I learned that he was an engineer with the rank of an SS Major. As I stood before him, I said in German, „I have a degree in engineering and would like some work which is more in line with my technical abilities."

It looked suddenly as though he was going to draw his weapon and shoot me on the spot to punish me for this impudence. But after a few juicy oaths, including „Accursed Jew!" and similar epithets, he asked me a bit more calmly, „You say, you are an engineering graduate?" „Jawohl!" I answered stiffly. The adjutant gave a curt order, „You will wash and make yourself a bit more human and come back in fifteen minutes, and I will bring you to my office!"

After I had washed my hands and splashed a little water over my face, I made my way to the office of Rudi, the SS-Major. „Where did you study? Where did you learn German? Can you do drafting? Can you read technical drawings? Can you develop a project?" After a pause I replied, „I have the same degree as you, Sir, only I earned it in France. You surely have more experience than I, but we have learned the same things!" Finally appeased, he commented merely, „I will send you to the planning office, and there you will take a technical examination!"

An SS-Adjutant took charge of me and told me to follow him. The technical office was located about two hundred meters from the Works in a very new building. As we entered, a large, already white-haired gentleman in civilian clothes approached us. I followed him to the third floor, where he admitted me to the planning office, which was equipped with every sort of device. Very correctly, he asked me to take a seat before a drawing board where I found pencils, erasers and everything I needed for drafting. He introduced himself, „Bosch, Chief Engineer, Directing Engineer of the Works!" Then he inquired as to my first name: - „Jakob!" - „Good, you will develop plans for the arrangement of the workplace! I think you know what you have to do! In two or three hours I will come back to see what you have accomplished!"

He closed the door behind him and left me alone. There I sat with my own thoughts for company. I had to think of something; it was a matter of life and death. Without losing a moment, I started working. After about three hours I thought, Now you have it! But no one came. I began to check everything again and correct possible errors. No one, still no one! No sound reached my ears! The more time went by, the more my anxiety grew. And what if someone had forgotten me? The silence began to drive me crazy. I attempted to detect even the slightest sound. Deathly still. I need not mention that I had had nothing to drink or eat, no chance to go to the toilet. Naturally I had no timepiece, but I could see that the day was coming to an end.

Suddenly I heard a key in the lock, and finally the door opened. Chief Engineer Bosch called to me, „Come, come, quick, quick, you are expected at the roll-call! Run fast so that you can still reach your group: To be honest - I forgot about you!" - „but," I begged him urgently, „Would you like to look at my work? I have long since finished everything!" - He cast a rapid glance at the work and said, „Everything in order! That is very nice, and I have already given my instructions. Tomorrow when you come to the Works, you will go directly to the technical office!" I had an urge to hug him out of gratitude, but he gave me no time for that. I ran down and emerged in front of the Works where my group was already preparing to move out.

In the block my comrades asked what had happened. „Very simple," I explained to them, „I believe I will work as a engineer in the planning office of the Weichsel-Union Metal Works!"* That was the new name of the works, which had previously been called the „Zaporoz'e Union Metal Works"; the pressure of the Soviet Army had forced the German Wehrmacht to withdraw from the Ukraine, and so they had transported the armament industries back to Poland. I was hungry, and this time I gladly consumed the meager evening meal, which consisted of a piece of black bread, a little margarine and a bit of cheese, everything washed down with a repulsive beverage which we called „tea."

On the next day after the endless roll-call in the cold of dawn, we got under way, and I went to my new job. Chief Engineer Bosch received me cordially, and I soon felt that we could even become friends. My duties were commensurate with my abilities, and from the start I felt comfortable in the respon-sible work which was assigned to me. The instructions were very specific: First I had to prepare a list of the various machines and in the appendix give precise information about their functions.

---

* September 30, 1943: „The Weichsel-Union Metal Works takes over from the military authorities of the KL Auschwitz an assembly plant and part of its machines and production facilities that Friedrich Krupp AG formerly rented. The Weichsel-Union Metal Works begins the assembly of several machines and the production of detonators." (D. Czech, *Kalendarium der Ereignisse im Konzentrationslager Auschwitz-Birkenau 1939-1945*, Reinbek and Frankfurt 1989, p. 616).

As I later found out, the Works had the task of producing grenades. Over three hundred men and women worked there, half on the day shift, the others during the night. The day and the night workers met only at the entrance of the Works, if everyone appeared at the same time. The march to and from the camp usually lasted more than half an hour.** If it rained, it was even more dismal, since we arrived at the barracks soaking wet. Even today, I ask myself how we found the strength to endure those interminable marches in rain, snow or terrible cold, which made the entire body stiff. And on top of that we were also supposed to sing.

On the other hand, I must admit that my working conditions were far more agreeable than those of most of my comrades who were assigned to the outside work detachments. But also in comparison to my comrades in the Works, I had the most attractive work, namely without any supervisor besides my boss, Chief Engineer Bosch.

Two or three days after he had taken me into the technical office, he summoned me and asked, „Tell me, Jakob, for what crime did they intern you, after all?“ - It took my breath away, and I dared to ask, „Do I look like a criminal?“ - „Of course not, but I don't understand that, for after all, there are only criminals in the KZs: If you broke no serious law, why did they send you here?“ - Then I attempted to explain that I was a Jew from Salonica and had lost my family in Auschwitz. - He pointed to the distant smokestacks and commented, „But here we are in an industrial zone!“ - I, of all persons, had to explain to him that the smokestacks belonged to crematoria where they burned the people who were gassed, and that my parents and the greatest share of the Jewish population of Salonica had been killed there. He admitted to being dumbfounded by these revelations, and then he added softly, „So that is the German culture!“

How was it possible that he did not know? I think that as an engineer he had had to accept his post there. Bosch was from Zaporoz'e; the munitions factory was under the control of the SS, and therefore it seemed to me that he was constantly on guard, for the SS also exercised its reign of terror against German civilians.

Otherwise, everything connected with the murders, above all the gas chambers and crematoria, was in the hands of the SS. All the work was carried out by prisoners, and these had no contact at all with the other prisoners, in order that

---

** October 16,1943: „In the works of the Weichsel-Union Metal Works are employed 3233 male prisoners, among them 305 as technicians, and 35 female prisoners from KL Auschwitz.“ (D. Czech, *Kalendarium der Ereignisse im Konzentrationslager Auschwitz-Birkenau 1939-1945*, Reinbek and Frankfurt 1989, p. 630).

nothing concerning their secret activities would become known outside the camps. Therefore, in the end, these prisoners were themselves sent to the gas chambers.

But, then, how did we find out? The reasons are simple. We never saw our family members again, nor anyone of those who after their arrival had to go to the right side. Furthermore, we saw that the SS culled out the weakest at each selection, those who were no longer able to work at the expected tempo. And these we likewise never saw again. The following warning became common knowledge, „Watch out that you do not lose weight, and stay fit for work; otherwise they'll send you up the smokestack to heaven!" The most frightening thing about the march to or from work was the stink of the ovens, which was nothing like the familiar smell of burnt industrial wastes.

After that initial discussion Chief Engineer Bosch and I became true friends. He made it clear to me that I must, naturally, tell no one about our conversations. Even after the technical office was increased to ten engineers and two or three draftsmen he continued to take me into his confidence.

6. Julie, Bella, imprisonment and acquittal

One ice-cold day I was relieving myself in our Works' latrine, while to my right and left, several comrades were similarly occupied. Suddenly, I heard a cry of joy from my right, „A Dio santo - my God, that is Jacques Stroumsa!" I turned around and recognized Marcel Matalon, a former comrade from Salonica. He embraced me with tears in his eyes. And as he saw that I was much better clad than he, he wanted to know whether I performed any function in the Works. Then he explained to me that he had been arrested in Marseilles where his family lived.

His work in the camp consisted in unloading coal wagons a few meters in front of the entrance to the Works. It was coal for the central heating system, which also served to provide an even temperature for the machines. He worked on the wagons in icy cold, „A few days more, and I will be a dead man!" - Without promising anything, I wrote down his prisoner number and block number, gave it to Chief Engineer Bosch and described our reunion to him. Two days later my friend Marcel was taken on at the Works as a mechanic.

The foreman, who was always friendly to us, assigned him to an automatic machine for thread cutting. He had to watch it constantly, service it and occasionally oil it. Another mutual friend, Freddy Allalouf, who unfortunately did not survive Mauthausen, worked beside him. During our entire confinement in

Auschwitz and up to the evacuation on the 18th of January, 1945, Marcel and Freddy were inseparable; they worked together, slept next to each other, ate together and together hoped for liberation.

I owe Chief Engineer Bosch an enormous debt of gratitude for his understanding. He promised to help me whenever possible, naturally with the condition that it did not endanger his own safety. Thus it happened that one day I learned of the arrival from Strassburg of a young rabbi with his wife and six children. When I spoke with Chief Engineer Bosch about my concern, he immediately arranged for the rabbi to be taken on by the Union. He was assigned to assembly, a boring but easy job. The poor rabbi, whom no one had told the truth about his family and their fate, kept asking me when he would finally be able to see his wife and children. I consoled him by saying that it was very difficult to arrange, but one had to keep hoping.

A former deportee from France, Raphael Esrail (He has already visited me in Jeruselem) recently wrote me a letter, „As for me, Liliane and I are especially happy to have found the man who succeeded in freeing a woman, one who had scarcely any chance of surviving, from the hell of Auschwitz." At that time I had arranged for this young girl to work in the factory. She became his wife and is still living today.

Chief Engineer Bosch also helped me to bring my sister Bella and her inseparable girlfriend Elisa to the Union when the so-called „Red Riding Hood Detachment," in which she worked, was dissolved. I had entirely forgotten this episode and only remembered it when Bella brought it up one day in Paris.

In the same manner, I was also able to rescue my dear sister Julie, who was a violinist in the women's orchestra of Birkenau. At home in Salonica my two-years younger sister Julie had also played the violin. One day, however, the entire orchestra was taken off to an unknown destination. After the liberation we learned that the orchestra had been sent to Bergen-Belsen. There, in the last days before the liberation, my sister fell victim to typhus.

Only once did I have the joy of seeing her again. Our soup was, as it happened, cooked in the women's camp; at my request, a girl from the soup transport switched jobs with my sister Julie, and so we got to see each other once more for half an hour, though we hardly dared to speak. I never saw her again.

*

In May 1986 I was working on the history of the Jewish deportation from Greece as a volunteer in a department of Yad Vashém. The day came for the dedication of the memorial to the resistance fighters of all countries. Our friend,

Shimshon Eden, had assigned me to lay a wreath at the foot of the monument, together with another ex-prisoner, Maurice Pioro, from Brussels. Pioro was the president of both the Deported Jewish Belgians and the Friends of Yad Vashém and a very congenial person. A few months after his return I received a touching letter from Brussels, which I would like to reprint in its full length; as the sole record of the time during which my sister Julie played in the orchestra, this is a remembrance of how a friend had known her:

Brussels, October 18, 1986

Dear Mr. Stroumsa!

I was very surprised to hear from Maurice Pioro that he had met the brother of „Little Julie." You are surely asking yourself why „Little Julie"? Well, we had two „Julies" in the orchestra. Both were Greek women from Salonica. I picked up the trail of „Big Julie" four years ago. She lived with her husband, Dr. Menache, in Miami, a man who was likewise a former orchestra member from Auschwitz. Unfortunately, she has since died. She belonged to the group of Greek women playing in the orchestra in which Lilly and Yvette, who now live in the USA, were also members.

As to your younger sister, I remember her as a very gentle, reserved girl who never took part in the sometimes heated discussions which we had. We all wanted, of course, to hold on tight to life, and so we imitated the reality outside in that we held comradely discussions. Julie was always neutral. She lacked the fighting nature to survive in those shoals of death.

I hope we will meet someday in Brussels or Jerusalem and embrace you warmly in memory of „Little Julie." (p.88)

Fanny Birkenwald

*

Block 10 in Auschwitz was reserved for the women who had to be made available for Dr. Mengeles' medical experiments. Between Block 10 and Block 11 there was a gloomy court, and at the end of the court the Black Wall, against which the firing squads executed prisoners. The „Bunker" was located in the basement of Block 11 and was a prison from which few prisoners ever emerged alive. I was also to experience this filthy bunker.

In the Works I had a Polish comrade, a Catholic, with whom I made friends. I slept near him in the Block. He was taken into custody in Cracow during the course of a razzia and nursed a burning hatred for the Germans, who had in this manner separated him from his family. As a political prisoner he had, however, a right to a food package every fourteen days, one which his mother regularly left at the control post at the entrance to the camp. Every time my friend received his package, he gave me a bar of chocolate, a lump of sugar or something sweet, which I very much enjoyed, but really wasn't supposed to accept.

I cannot claim that I was ever hungry during the eighteen months which I spent in the Union; for I had, after all, no physical labor to perform and could thus survive on the meager rations I received. My work was not much different from what it was in peacetime. The terrible difference was confinement in the concentration camp. In the office, we occasionally learned something from Chief Engineer Bosch of the military developments at the fronts. Thus, for example, we all celebrated the day the Allies landed in Normandy (June 6, 1944) as a day of joy, which promised us the end of the war. But what end did the SS have planned for us? Would they also send us up the smokestack someday, like millions of others? Or would the Russian offensive advance so swiftly that they would free us from the grasp of our executioners before the latter had enough time to liquidate us?

One evening my Polish comrade said, after he had once more received an ample package from his mother, „Jakob, you may feel free to accept what I give you, that is surely little enough! And already you are invited to visit me after the liberation! You will see piles of splendid things: good roasts that my mother will prepare and many other tasty things! Here, I will give you my address!" He scribbled his name and address in Poland on a slip of paper, which I promptly stuck into my jacket pocket.

A few days later another friend came to tell me that my younger sister Bella marched past our Works every morning with her comrades. They called her workplace 'Canada' (used as a synonym to signify great riches because of the money often found in the linings of the clothes), because there they sorted the clothes which the deportees had to remove before going to the gas chambers. The women of the detachment were called „Red Riding Hoods" (Rotkäppchen) because they wore red scarves. After the liberation, my younger sister Bella told me that she and her friend Elisa had once found a thousand dollar bill. Despite her deathly fear, she hid this valuable bill until she found a Polish master from the camp to whom she could pass it. In return, every day for almost six months he supplied them with tasty buttered bread with salami, which they secretly wolfed down.

*

I had permission to take a direct route from the Works to the planning office and back, which was about 200 meters in all. The path which the Red Riding Hoods used was located about 100 meters to the right. Without hesitating, I approached the girls as I saw the detachment going by. In fact, I discovered my sister Bella, and from afar we waved to each other. How gladly I would have taken her in my arms, but my common sense restrained me.

Just at this moment it happened that an SS-man was passing by. He knew me well, at least by sight, for he was an ethnic German technician and assigned to monitor the mechanical workshop, which was manned by both Poles and Germans. - „What are you doing there, then?" he asked me. - „I only wanted to see my sister, who was marching past in her Red Riding Hood detachment: Since our arrival in Auschwitz six months ago, that was the first time that I could at least see her!" - He ordered me gruffly to precede him to the Works.

There I had to go into his small office, „First empty your pockets and place the contents on my desk!" he ordered. He carefully examined everything till his face suddenly lighted up, „Now I have you!" he cried and unfolded a slip - the address of my Polish friend, „You wanted to escape from Auschwitz, you filthy little Yid! There is the proof that I have already long sought!"

Without listening to my explanations, he made several phone calls and ordered me to follow him to the exit of the Works. There a small military vehicle awaited us, and a few minutes later we were at the entrance to the camp, directly before the infamous entry slogan, „Arbeit macht frei."

The camp at Auschwitz was surrounded by a double barbed wire fence. Between the two fences there was a considerable space. The fences carried 6,000 volts of electricity. One didn't need to be an electrical engineer to know that this fence was deadly, if one touched it. Several of our unfortunate comrades put an end to their suffering by throwing themselves against this fence.

Arriving at the inner entrance gate, the SS-man on duty opened the heavy lock of the side door, which led into the no-man's-land between the two barbed-wire fences, shoved me in and said scornfully, „Now you can commend your soul to all the saints! Remain standing and wait until someone brings you out!" He turned the key in the lock and strode off, laughing derisively.

There was nothing for me to do but to wait. On both sides 6,000 volts. I held out, not moving at all. After a few hours the same SS-man came back to open the door. I had to march in front of him, he led me into the Bunker of Block 11 and handed me over to the „Bunker Porter," whose job it was to administer punishments through beatings or perform executions by hanging.

He was a Jew, and according to rumor, a former trainer of Max Schmeling.* One needed only to look at him to lose all courage: This Hercules could have crushed me with a single blow of his fist. He opened a cell, and unbidden I crept inside. It was almost totally dark, dank and cold. I crouched in a corner, daring not to think. How could I ever get out of here again? I feared that I had reached the end of the line.

Two, three hours later - a click, the door was opened and a beam of light pierced the cell. „Here catch," cried the executioner and threw me a loaf of bread larger than any I had seen for a long time. Besides that, he gave me a blanket, „You shouldn't freeze! Have no fear, we will get you out of here somehow!" The heavy door was locked. There I sat, alone again, and wolfed down the dry bread. The events of the day must have exhausted me, for I dozed off wrapped tightly in the blanket. In my terrible misery I had to spend still another day there and counted the hours as they passed.

On the next day, when the first scanty beams of sunlight fell in the cell, the door was opened again. „Jakob," said the executioner, „get ready, you must go before the Court! Watch out that you defend yourself well!" An SS-man led me to the Court, in another barrack on the opposite end of the camp. In Auschwitz I had already experienced the most absurd and contradictory situations: the orchestra, in which I played first violin; the hospital, where my ruptured hernia was operated on, an inflammation of the lungs from which I almost died, the Bunker, where I was locked in for two nights and now the „Court." I was prepared for anything.

A young SS-man asked me correctly whether I needed an interpreter. „No, I speak very good German!" Calmly I answered all further questions. Really, I had never thought of escaping. I explained that my homeland, Greece, was very far away and I was waiting for the end of the war to return home. I made no reference to the gas chambers, but rather emphasized that I worked in the engineering office and had only tried to see my younger sister, who was passing by, as I had not seen her for six months. And the slip of paper with the address of my Polish comrade? That was an invitation to Cracow after the war was finally over.

The unbelievable happened. After a consultation, the Court really did let me go free, sent me to work and even permitted me a day of rest in the Block (see pp. 98-99).

---

* Jakov Kozelczuk, the so-called „Bunkerjakob," denied by Max Schmeling; cf. among others H. Langbein 1972, p. 215.

*

In 1986 I visited Auschwitz with my youngest daughter, Florence-Margalith. At the entrance gate to Auschwitz we were all deeply shaken. My daughter cried. To the left of the entrance I again saw a few two-story red brick houses, which at that time belonged to the SS administration. I read a sign „Archi-vum, - Ar-chive," and my friend Jacky Handeli, who accompanied us, suggested that we should go in. In the second story a very polite employee wrote down our KZ numbers and said, „Come back afterwards, then you will receive copies of your documents!"

The documents (in the appendix of this book) show that I was apparently in good health on my arrival in Birkenau on May 9, 1943, aside from the fact that I lacked four teeth. The judgment which was handed down on February 16, 1944, and set me „free" granted me a day of rest in the Block. This document bears my signature and underneath that of the SS-Unterscharführer and the judge, whose names I did not bother trying to decipher.

In 1986 a work appeared in New York with important contemporary historical research under the title *Secretaries of Death*, published by our friend and fellow-sufferer, Dr. Lore Shelley, Ph.D., who sent a copy to me in Jerusalem. I showed her my documents from the Polish Archive administration at Auschwitz, and immediately she deciphered the signature in question as that of Klaus Dylewski, member of the camp Gestapo. Her book includes a few details of his life (p. 361). First arrested in April 1959, he was convicted of war crimes in Frankfurt in August 1965.* However, he had saved my life in Auschwitz when he sent me back to my work.

7. Death march and rescue in Mauthausen

Life in Auschwitz was going on 'normally' at the end of 1944.** To be sure, the SS-men seemed a little nervous, for it was probably also clear that fate would

---

* He was found guilty „of assistance in the joint murder in at least thirty-two cases, in each of two of these cases cases committed against at least seven hundred-fifty persons" and sentenced to a „total punishment of five years imprisonment." (B. Naumann 1965, p. 516 and 518, cf. also pp. 23, 52, 492, 508, 529, 546; cf. also H. Langbein 1972, pp. 208, 326, 466, 566, 570).

** October 10, 1944: In the Women's Camp Auschwitz I, three female prisoners who worked in the Weichsel-Union Metal Works are arrested. They were Ella Gärtner, Ester Wajsblum and Regina Safin. They are accused of having stolen explosives from the Work's magazine and given them to the prisoners of the Special Detachments. These explosives enabled the prisoners to construct primitive grenades which they used during the unrest on October 7." - December 30, 1944: „The labor force of Women's Camp Auschwitz consisted of 6,015 female prisoners. Of them 840 are ill and unable to work ... 1,090 [work] in the Weichsel-Union

take an evil turn for them. The war would surely soon be over. In the technical office of the Union we were very well informed. The Allies had already landed; the troops were moving in the direction of Paris, not only from Belgium, but also from Holland. The Germans resisted, but slowly they fell back. In our vicinity the pressure of the Soviet military machinery grew stronger and stronger. We were convinced that we would be freed by the Red Army. Nevertheless nothing happened, and the work went on.

In December 1944 we began, however, to notice that the camp was becoming less important. In the evening, as we came back from the Union, we had no doubt that there were fewer men around the barracks than before: The camp was emptying itself while we were working. Fear overwhelmed us. What had happened to our comrades? Had they been taken elsewhere or liquidated? We suddenly received an answer to these troubling questions: After the roll call one evening when, as usual, we returned from the Union, we received a brief order, „In twenty minutes everyone will assemble here!"

We imagined that now the anticipated transport awaited us. The Russians were thus too late to free us, and the SS had time to drag us to another location. Marcel Matalon, my friend from Salonica, was extremely agitated, „Jacques, I know I cannot march very far in this cold; I will hide in the hospital because there are already a few Greeks there!" - „Marcel," I said, „God protect you! Only I greatly fear that the SS-men will come and drive you out with their dogs and weapons, but naturally I will not try to dissuade you!" With tears in his eyes, he hastily embraced me and left.

I had brought Marcel Matalon into the Union with the help of Chief Engineer Bosch, and we had spent almost a year together. Eight days after we were led away he was rescued by the Russians and brought back to Marseilles. I met him in there August 1945, and he prepared a princely reception for me. He put everything he possessed at my disposal, above all his apartment. Unfortunately it did not turn out so well for my friend Freddy Allalouf; he went with us and died of dysentery soon after our arrival in Mauthausen.

On January 19, 1945, toward six o'clock p.m., on a pitch-dark evening, we passed for the last time through the gate of Auschwitz. We were in no way equipped to march for a long time in the cold and snow, unlike the SS-men, who escorted us on both sides and continually cried, „Quick, quicker!" We had to keep up a rapid pace, and from time to time a shot rang out. Anyone who stopped for any reason was mercilessly shot down. With my right arm I supported a

---

Metal Works." (D. Czech, *Kalendarium der Ereignisse im Konzentrationslager Auschwitz-Birkenau 1939-1945*, Reinbek and Frankfurt 1989, pp. 902 and 953).

comrade and did not let go of him. Suddenly I heard a shot directly behind us, and my friend said in Spanish, „No te aboltes - Don't turn around!" Again one of us had been shot. Under these sad circumstances the motto was „March or die!"

It is incomprehensible what people can endure! Our ordeal was to continue for six days and seven nights. The last stage was spent in covered transport wagons, and on January 25, 1945, we arrived in a miserable state at the depot of Mauthausen. The death march had lasted all too long.

I will never forget what happened next. It was the early morning hours: the inhabitants, who saw us leaving the train, crossed themselves and quickly closed the windows, so frightful was the scene. Almost all of us had diarrhea because there was nothing to eat except snow. We did not, of course, know Mauthausen, but we were acquainted with the evil reputation of the stone quarry there. We knew that prisoners were thrown down from above, and that in this manner they met a terrible death.[*]

We climbed out of the wagons and marched in rows of five for about five kilometers to the camp. Auschwitz was terrible, but anyone who has not seen Mauthausen knows only half of the KZ reality. The camp was literally a fortress. Within was a large, snow-covered square. They sent us to boiling hot showers; afterwards we had to reassemble stark naked on the large square. I do not know how long it lasted. I only know that they finally led us to a barrack where they clothed us scantily and gave everyone a blanket. Then they brought us to another large barrack which was open on all sides. To anyone watching this scene, we must have looked like ghosts.

It was there that I experienced a scene which could not have been more gruesome. A few SS-men guarded us. Suddenly, a prisoner turned sobbing to them and complained, „Someone stole my blanket!" The SS-man turned and asked, „Who?" The prisoner pointed, and then I witnessed something incredibly inhuman. The SS-man pulled his weapon, aimed at this man and shot him in the face. I recognized him at once as David, the tool maker from the Union, now just a lifeless mass that tumbled to the ground and was kicked outside by the guards. Like most of the specialists in the Union, David was a kindly and decent person who did not deserve to die in such a senseless manner for a theft which he certainly had not committed. As we watched, we became more and more terrified.

The day finally came to an end. They sent us to another barrack which filled at once. No one knew whether that was a good or bad sign. There I discovered

---

[*] Cf. G. Rabitsch, „The KL Mauthausen." In: *Studien zur Geschichte der Konzentrationslager*, Stuttgart 1970, pp. 59 and 65.

my dear cousin, Guillaume Yahiel, who had wasted away to a skeleton. He hurried to me and threw himself sobbing into my arms. It was our first reunion since our deportation from Salonica. But we could not speak to each other. We were too exhausted by our emotions.

*

I no longer remember under what circumstances I suddenly heard the chap from the *Stubendienst* roar out my number in Polish: „121097!" I went to him and indicated who I was. „Ah," he said, „we have been looking for you. You are supposed to go as an engineer to the Messerschmitt aircraft works!" - „But I understand nothing of airplanes!" - „No matter, you are supposed to be good at drafting!" My records from the Union had apparently arrived, so I had to go back to work.

The foremen were Austrian civilians. I knew that after the *Anschluss* the Austrians had prepared a triumphal reception for Hitler and was therefore very mistrustful. Nevertheless, after one or two months people became more talkative. Thus I heard that the allied armies were advancing on all sides. One day a foreman with whom I had the best contacts said to me, „Jakob, you must have no more fear, the war will soon be over; then you can return to your homeland and your family!"

I looked at him sadly. He did not know that I had no family left - that my young, pregnant wife, her mother, her father, my mother, my father had immediately after our arrival all been murdered in the gas chamber and burnt in the crematorium. I only hinted about it, for I had not forgotten my confinement in the Bunker of Auschwitz. I had learned - all too painfully - that one never knew with whom one was dealing.

The days passed. Only God could know what our fate would be. One morning, toward the end of April (1945), the SS sent us not to the Works, but to another camp, which was situated a few kilometers away and which would soon be the site of great jubilation. In the center of the court there was a solitary water faucet. Since our march from Auschwitz I had made the friendship of a nice young chap from Salonica, a true philosopher named Jacques Choel, a plumber by profession. He had survived thanks to his skill and technical knowledge. We slept side by side and took our meager meals together.

We were now sure that the end of the war was imminent. We debated endlessly and asked ourselves again and again about our chances of survival. Now we had the impression that our chances were improving each day because the SS had suddenly disappeared. We had discovered that our guards were older men who wore Wehrmacht helmets, perhaps farmers from neighboring villages. We also noticed that they came by bicycle, perhaps in order to be able to escape more quickly when our liberators arrived.

*

One afternoon we were at the water faucet occupied with cleaning our undergarments when one of us let out a cry of joy, „The guards are gone!" They had left behind their uniforms and weapons in the watchtower. The unbelievable had happened! Despite our great joy, my friend Choel and I maintained our calm.

Toward evening we heard a dull droning, then powerful tanks rolled up to the main gate of the camp, „Are they French, English or American?" - „Hard to say!" - We ran up the street through the wide open gate. The brave soldiers, our liberators, threw cigarettes to us, I caught one or two Lucky Strikes and knew they were Americans! That was on the 8th of May, 1945, at six o'clock in the evening.

Choel and I were so exited that we began to cry. Our joy, however, could hardly overcome our despair. Those of us who had been dragged from our homes with mothers, fathers, sisters and brothers and wives and children were now alone. What was left of our families? We decided not to go into the street in the night. To be sure we had eaten almost nothing, but despite our gnawing hunger, we refused to eat raw meat, which our comrades offered us. They had plundered the stocks of provisions and could not even muster the patience to prepare the meat. More than anything we needed sleep, but where?

*

In the last few days some of us, exhausted from all our privations, had gone to sleep never to rise again. The barracks were full of their corpses, but we lacked the strength to carry them out. The situation was inconceivably tragic. Jacques Choel, the tall one, bent over so that I could climb on his shoulders and boost myself onto a rafter. That is where we spent our first night in freedom.

When morning came, Choel awakened me with the news that he was suffering from a high fever. If you want to save me, take me to a hospital!" I held his hand and we went out into the street. I supported him with great effort as we walked for almost two kilometers. Then I saw a school marked as a hospital. We entered, and female soldiers (WACs) received us in a friendly manner. It was clear what was wrong with Jacques Choel, „He has typhus," said a pretty girl with the rank of lieutenant. My poor Jacques began to howl, „*No me deshes, me vo a muerir*! Don't leave me in the lurch, otherwise I will die!" The WAC turned to me, „What's the matter with you?" I asked for permission to remain, she came over to me, raised my eyelid, looked me straight in the eye and assured me, „Yes, you can stay, because you are just as sick as your friend!"

A happy fate had drawn us to this emergency hospital which the American army had set up in the vicinity of 'Gusen II', and with the aid of antibiotics our recovery progressed relatively quickly. During this period an officer visited me one day. „Don't you have anyone in the USA whom I could notify of your liberation from the Nazi camps?" No, I had no one. But I wracked my brains, and suddenly I remembered the man whom we had already regarded as my sister Julie's fiancee, David Perahia from Brooklyn.

Before the war David and his mother had come to Salonica to hold the wedding there. He wanted to see my father, whose pupil he had once been, and we had welcomed them warmly. I believe that it was love at first sight between David and my sister Julie, who didn't want to be separated from each other. David had sent us all the necessary forms from New York in order for Julie to come to him, but the official formalities took time. The American Consulate in Salonica finally refused to provide a visa with the excuse that the USA would soon declare war on the Axis powers, which did in fact occur. Everything else, including my sister's engagement, became irrelevant.

The American officer sent a telegram to David Perahia in Brooklyn, and he wired me one hundred Dollars. At that time I still did not know of my sister's tragic fate. Only some months later did we learn that she had died of typhus in Bergen-Belsen, only a few days before the liberation.

*

Years later, I owed my reunion with David Perahia to pure chance. In Jerusalem a mutual friend had told me that David and his wife had retired and moved to Miami, which was not exactly in our vicinity. In November 1990 I received an invitation from the office of the United Nations in New York to fly to Quito in Ecuador in order to install the lighting for the historical city center.

At two o'clock in the morning, I took off from Tel Aviv and was supposed to arrive in Quito on the same day at eight-thirty in the evening. My wife Laura wanted to accompany me, and we made every effort to find seats on the same flight. Everything was proceeding as planned until we were supposed to change planes in Miami. The logistics were so complicated that we missed our connection to Quito. But sometimes there is fortune in misfortune.

I called David right away from the hotel, and he was speechless with excitement. A taxi brought us to Miami Beach. How should I describe our reunion? David was already close to eighty-five years old; the last time we had seen each other was in 1938, even before the war. Fifty-two years had gone by in the meantime. I was a bit afraid to remind him of the past. With admirable strength he even showed me a photo album from that time. I relived the most beautiful memories of my family, of my father, my mother, my brother and friends, and especially Julie, who had all been swallowed up by the hell of Auschwitz.

*

As soon as we had recovered from the typhus and after a few days of rest, we were taken to another American military camp. Here the former deportees and forced laborers were assembled according to nationality. We Greeks were worst off, not because of the treatment, which was extremely good and equal for all, but because the Americans could not send us back to our country. The war between Italy and Yugoslavia over Triest was not yet over, and each of the two powers laid claim to the city.

A Greek Orthodox comrade, who had been drafted for forced labor, gave me a piece of good advice, as he commented, „Jacques, you have a command of several foreign languages, above all French, because you studied in France: Thirty kilometers from here in a small city there is a French consulate; I am sure that they would permit you to travel to Paris, if you explain your problem to them!"

After the camp leader had permitted me to go there, I quickly located the consulate and was introduced to a young French lieutenant, who supervised the office of the consulate. Since I possessed no identification papers, I had to answer his many, very kindly posed questions. Then he embraced me cordially with the words, „Monsieur, I will obtain French citizenship for you tomorrow. You are warmly welcome among us!" During our conversations, he had discovered that we had attended the same faculty at the University of Bordeaux where I obtained an engineering degree in radio-telegraphy in 1935 and he in 1939! For the first time, after so many years, someone had addressed me as „Monsieur." I would have to learn what it meant to be treated like a human being again.

8. New life and sorrow as a permanent state

The French prepared a touching reception upon my return to Paris, and I began to believe that I could start a new life. Nevertheless I continued to be troubled by my situation. The war had brutally robbed me of everything. Who could replace the love of my mother, the warm affection of my father, brother, sisters, the love of my young wife Nora? Although my grief began to become permanent, with a heavy heart I made every effort to resume a normal life.

One day I happened to stroll with no particular aim through the streets of Paris, more precisely through the St. Germain-des-Près. My glance was attracted to a shop window, and I found myself standing before a famous shop, „Martin Violins," rue de Vaugirard. The violins which I saw before me were so stunningly beautiful that suddenly all my memories flooded back ... Salonica, the Conservatoire Grecos, my violin teacher, Livio Marchesini, the Maccabi and finally Auschwitz-Birkenau. Unbelievable, what had happened in such a few years! Without reflecting I entered the shop, where a young woman promptly asked me what I wanted.

„I would like to see a violin," I said in a small voice. She handed me a violin and bow and invited me to examine them. While I was still tuning the violin I sensed she was observing me. Even today I recall vividly how I then played the first measures of Mozart's A-major concerto - as I had once before in Auschwitz.

Totally astonished, the woman asked me, „Where do you come from, originally?" - „I have just spent two years in Auschwitz." - „Were you deported from France?" - „No from my native city of Salonica." - „And where did you learn French so well?"

While I briefly told my story, the young woman wrote out a bill, „The violin with case and spare strings, that comes to 1,300 francs!" - „That is unfortunately impossible for me, for I possess only 1,000 francs, which I was given by the French government when I crossed the border." - Without hesitating she replied, „Then take everything for 1,000 francs! My husband, who is still in the army, will be pleased to hear that I could make you happy!"

In July 1945 this violin was my only joy. I have carefully saved it up until today for my granddaughter Dafna, the youngest daughter of Guy and Sara. From day to day it becomes increasingly clear that she has talent.

*

In August 1945 I began to work as an engineer in the planning office of the Sciacy Works in a suburb of Paris. On the third day the director informed me that at the express wish of my colleagues the firm wanted to present me with a month-long vacation in Nice. I could scarcely believe this generous offer and thanked him warmly, without, of course, accepting the sum of money placed at my disposal; for the French government's „Carte de Repatrié" already guaranteed me certain privileges, including free trips and accommodations.

In Paris, Greeks were accustomed to gathering during the evenings in a locale of the 'Agence Juive' on the rue Guy-Patin, to exchange news of family members and friends. My approaching trip was quite an event, and friends advised me to visit Marseilles first, because numerous Greeks were waiting there for a ship which was to bring them home, „Perhaps there you will even find someone from your family! They always meet in the Café Pierre, close to the Prefecture!"

Arriving in Marseilles at seven-thirty in the morning with my borrowed suitcase, I descended the monumental staircase of the Gare Saint Charles and crossed the Boulevard d'Athènes in the direction of Cannebière. How many times I had passed this way as a student in 1930 because the faculty of natural sciences was located immediately behind the train station. In the vicinity of the „Hôtel de Noailles" I suddenly imagined that I was seeing a vision! There in the flesh was Marcel Matalon approaching me! We had last seen each other in Auschwitz on January 18, 1945. At that time, Marcel had hidden himself in the sick-bay. A week later he was freed by the Russians and repatriated to Marseilles by way of Sevastapol. As he took the suitcase out of my hand, he asked at once what I wanted for breakfast. I replied, „A good milk coffee and warm croissants! And then bring me as quickly as possible to Café Pierre, to the meeting place of the Greeks from Salonica."

*

It was during this brief stay in Marseilles that I met the woman with whom I would share the rest of my life - Laura Saporta. She had been deported with her parents, who held Spanish passports, from Athens to Bergen-Belsen. Her mother, a Camhi from Monastir, had died in the camp from the after-effects of dysentery. Her father, who came from Salonica, lay in a surgical clinic, severely ill with cancer. That first time we met, Laura wore a kerchief, because her hair had not yet grown back. Like me, she had suffered from typhus at the time of the liberation. All the misfortunes that had befallen us served to bind us together.

Following the death of her father on the first of September in 1945, I asked Laura to come to Paris for a few days before she returned to her family in Athens. After the prescribed (by Jewish tradition) seven days of mourning, she accepted my invitation and took a room in Hôtel Dacia on the Boulevard St. Michel, where some of her friends of the deportation period were already staying. With her good manners and simple charm, Laura conquered the hearts of my Parisian friends, and they immediately adopted her into their circle. Everyone advised me to dissuade her from returning to Greece and to marry her instead. I naturally wanted very much to marry her, but I lacked the means to support a family. A few days later, we agreed that we both had the same wish, but nevertheless decided to delay our marriage. Laura returned to Athens, and for an entire year we had to be content with exchanging letters.

Continuing to work at the Sciacy Works, I met Madame Baruch, the secretary of the Jewish aid organization O.S.E. (*Oeuvre de secours aux enfants juifs*), who introduced me to a psychologist. He advised me to resume my studies. It had always been my desire to complete my studies at the École Supérieur d'Électricité, which I could, however, not afford to do before the war. Now this dream was finally within reach.

On the basis of my earlier acquired diplomas, I was admitted not only to study, but the O.S.E. also assumed all financial obligations and, in addition, guaranteed me a scholarship. So on 5 November 1945 I became a student once again and could now devote myself exclusively to my studies.

*

Best of all, at last Laura and I could finally marry. A large wedding was of course out of the question, especially since the loss of our respective extended families was sadly apparent. After the civil ceremony, the religious ceremony took place on February 8, 1947, in the Sephardic Synagogue, in the Temple Brith Shalom. But the Israeli community was not in the position to provide for penniless ex-deportees, lacking families, who were unable to pay the usual fees. Thanks to the generous aid of Rabbi Cassorla and the well-known Cantor Popo, the formalities were simplified as much as possible and so in the end we did receive the solemn blessings for our marital bond.

We especially noticed how much we missed our families when our oldest son was born. The rite of circumcision was to be performed after eight days, but the Mohel demanded a sum of money which exceeded my monthly income. Fortunately, greatly angered by the behavior of the Mohel my friend Ady Steg helped me out of the pinch. As an internist in the Hospital Rothschild, he suggested that we bring the baby to him, and he himself performed the circumcision, exactly according to the requirements of our religious tradition.

As our financial position slowly improved, the emotional problems which our deportation had caused became increasingly clear. I had never stopped talking about them within our family. Naturally, the number on my forearm did not go unnoticed. Our son Guy was the first with whom we spoke. He was so affected that as a present for his Bar-Mitzvah he requested a trip to Israel. In August

1961, we were able to fulfill this wish. Despite the intense summer heat, we got to know the country well.

Coincidentally, the trial of Adolf Eichmann for crimes against humanity was being conducted at that time in Jerusalem and was being followed by the entire world. Guy was very interested, and we were able to observe parts of the trial from a side room. Our knowledge of Hebrew was not sufficient to understand the details, but we were very impressed by how the trial was proceeding and also read the commentaries in the French papers and the English-language *Jerusalem Post*.

After returning to Paris, it became increasingly clear to us that we would one day go to Israel to participate in the building of the country, insofar as it would be possible for us. Guy astonished us one day when he informed us that he now wanted to live as a believing, practicing Jew. This decision naturally turned the whole family upside down, because it forced us to follow the rules of Kashrut, the Jewish dietary laws (kosher). Finally, Guy, who was barely eighteen years old, set off for Israel with a student group, learned Hebrew in an accelerated course and enrolled in the philosophical faculty of the Hebrew University of Jerusalem. He had found his vocation.

*

In the meantime, I had accepted a position with a technical project in Algeria and in May 1967 we were living in Blida. A short time later, Nasser blockaded the Suez Canal and prepared for war against Israel. Outside the window of my office I saw the intense reactions of the Algerians who sat in the coffee houses bordering the Place Centrale. Algeria soon announced its readiness to fight on the side of Egypt against „the Zionist enemy." They mobilized and closed the airports while on television they showed terrible pictures of the imminent destruction of the state of Israel by the Arab armies, who were ready to fight for their „holy cause." We wanted above all to be reunited with Guy in Israel as soon as possible, but we were in a bind.

I had only holidays free. The General Secretary responded to my first request by informing us that my wife and our two daughters could leave the country at any time, but not I, for as a higher-level employee I had been „mo-bilized." I protested and showed the Auschwitz tattoo on my left forearm. I exclaimed, „Look, I lived through Auschwitz, and now you want to mobilize me for the war against Israel?!" The General Secretary left the room and came back ten minutes later with official papers authorizing me to leave the country.

On May 31, 1967, we left Algeria on board an old-fashioned Russian propeller airplane, which gave us a bumpy ride to Athens. When we arrived, our dear cousin Saby Camhi took charge. Aunt Viktorine urged us to leave our girls in Athens, and indicated that she would be willing to help us get to Tel Aviv.

In Greece, it was obvious that war was going to break out. Ships were no longer departing for Israel. With the help of his connections, Saby managed to obtain two seats for the next day, a Friday, on the last Alitalia flight. We landed in Tel Aviv toward ten in the evening with a military transport. The airport was wrapped in total darkness. Blue paper had been pasted over all windows. The atmosphere reeked of war.

Nevertheless, we were happy to be in Israel at last. But how could we get in touch with Guy? The next day our relatives Mario and Frida drove us to Jerusalem. It was the Sabbath and very difficult to maneuver through the streets jammed with military vehicles. Enormous armored vehicles were under way, and many soldiers were going to their units. War was imminent. How could we inform Guy that we had arrived?

In the vicinity of his apartment, someone advised us to park the car and continue on foot because it was the Sabbath. Finally we found Guy's apartment, but no one answered the doorbell. A neighbor who knew Guy opened his door and explained the situation. The University had already been closed for a week, and all students who could not be mobilized had been called to the kibbutzim so that they could replace the men who had already been called up. Guy was in the North of the country at Kibbutz Gonen, directly on the Syrian border. It was almost impossible to telephone on the Sabbath, so we drove back to Tel Aviv. In the meantime it had become even more difficult to travel. The streets were totally jammed and the heat unbearable.

Laura and I experienced the Six Day War in Tel Aviv, and Guy, whom we finally reached, was with us. I regarded it as my duty to volunteer for service in a technical detachment, perhaps with electrical work. I registered in Tel Aviv, my abilities were noted down, and I was asked to return the next day. Everyday for five days I dutifully returned to the office. On the sixth day I was informed that the war was over and was thanked for my willingness to help.

At home, I found Guy in tears. One of his young professors had been killed in action. We were shocked. This was the hour of our decision. We would remain in Israel!

*

„Whoever was in Auschwitz will never come out again. Nor will anyone who was not in Auschwitz will ever go there." I do not know who wrote these lines, but they are so important to me that they cross my mind again and again, and gradually it almost seems to me that they are my own.

Sorrow has become a permanent state with me. I feel sorrow for my closest relatives - father, mother, sister and brother, for my wife, parents-in-law and all relatives - a great number, so that it is very difficult to speak about them. I bear this sorrow alone, and I will bear it to the end. I do not weep often, but the loss of my family brought me pain from which I can never recover.

The destruction of the Jewish community of Salonica was horrible, but I do not suffer from this loss as much, because after the deportation I never lived there again. On every visit to Greece I naturally feel myself obligated to visit Salonica. I always stay in the 'Hotel Amalia', across from the Stoa Modiano, because there is no one left with whom I could stay. I always wake up very early and sit on the balcony in order to gaze at the sea. I smoke cigarette after cigarette in fear that I may start to weep. A Greek Orthodox friend once met me alone toward midnight and said, „I understand you, Jacques, you no longer know where you should go in Salonica, the city in which you once knew every stone." And that is the truth.

These days I often sit listening to my sixteen-year-old granddaughter, Daf-na, play the violin at home in Jerusalem. I remember myself at the same age playing in Salonica. How could I have imagined then that my love for this small, and yet so very powerful, instrument would one day save my life?

James Stuart Brice: Translator's Afterword

I wish first of all to express my appreciation for the opportunity provided by Professor Wiehn to work on Dr. Stroumsa's deeply moving book. I believe it is still Quite fitting that it appears about one year after the fiftieth anniversary of the liberation of Auschwitz. Asked about the fiftieth anniversary of Auschwitz, the Nobel laureate Elie Wiesel stated, "I think it is important to be there, to clarify what is important, to show the centrality of the Jewish experience, of total death and limited survival."* Dr. Stroumsa has surely made a worthwhile contribution here to this task.

Aside from the author, the most important person involved in producing this book was naturally Professor Wiehn. Without his patient work in planning and managing the project, it would not have been carried out. Since the author lives in Jerusalem, the various drafts had to be sent back and forth, along with requests for changes, additional text and suggestions for improvements. This was all taken care of by Professor Wiehn, just as he did in preparing the German edition with Brigitte Pimpl. He has unselfishly and unstintingly dedicated himself to the task of preserving the memories of survivors of the Holocaust for the historical record. Since this generation is now in the autumn of life, this means a race against present time to preserve the memories of past time from being lost forever. It must also be remembered that he has several book projects in the works at this time, along with a heavy workload as Professor of Sociology at the University of Konstanz, Germany. Not to be overlooked is also the great contribution of Professor Wiehn's wife, Mirjam, to furthering his historical projects.

Dr. Stroumsa has produced an excellent book of memoirs, written in a clear, modest and direct style. There is no attempt to embellish the story with pretentious literary or rhetorical techniques and no ideological framework. Although a highly educated person, he is not a professional historian, journalist or academic. Rather, he presents events as he experienced them. Hopefully this quality has not been obscured by my translation. This was based on the excellent German version by Brigitte Pimpl and Professor Wiehn. Deserving of great praise is the proofreading of the drafts which Dr. Stroumsa provided. If there is any fault in the book, it is that the author has told too little. One would like to know much more about the variety of different persons and events described. Perhaps in the future the author can find time from his busy schedule to add more details to the book.

---

* St. Paul Pioneer Press, 20 January 1995.

While I have not as yet made the acquaintance of Dr. Stroumsa, through reading and translating his book I feel almost as though I know him personally. He comes across in the text as a sensitive and humane person, deeply devoted to his family and possessed of a fine sense of humor. One must also admire his courage during his imprisonment and being able to start his life anew after the liberation. Few people with less inner strength and self-control would have been able to survive his experiences. As well, his dedication to both science and music show a high level of intelligence and culture. Knowing how hard it is to master even one foreign language or adapt to a single foreign country, we must admire him for the variety of different languages he is at home with (Greek, Ladino, Hebrew, French, German, English and perhaps others as well) and the number of countries where he has lived and worked. Likewise, knowing how hard it is to study at any university, let alone a foreign one, we must admire his having studied successfully at universities in France, Greece and Israel. Knowing how hard it is to acquire even rudimentary skills on any musical instrument, one must admire his mastery of the most beautiful and difficult of musical instruments. Knowing how difficult it is to cope with the minor difficulties of life in countries accustomed to peace and prosperity, one must admire him for having overcome his own trials and given solace to others in incomparably different times.

An especially positive aspect of the author's character is the balanced attitude he displays in the book. He is able to mention small acts of fairness or kindness, even by the workers in the camps. For example, the court which found him innocent of trying to escape, the cigarettes that an SS-man slipped him, the operation which the Polish surgeon performed on him or the orderly who saved his life during a selection. In contrast, many of the people victimized by lesser injustices are unable to maintain any sense of perspective regarding what has happened to them. We see this in the attitudes of many people caught up in the Yugoslavian conflict and other contemporary struggles. And how many of us could maintain the same sense of fairness as the author, should we be placed in comparable situations?

There are massive bibliographies of literature on the Holocaust, and one might well ask if there is really need for any more. Do new books and articles add anything essential to our knowledge? For many reasons there is a need for more to be written about this topic. There seems to be increased anti-Semitism since the end of the Cold War. Many people go so far as to deny that there even was a Holocaust. The majority may, of course, be narrow-minded persons trying to glorify the past or fanatic members of marginal hate groups. Some, however, are seemingly well-integrated into the community and otherwise apparently intelligent persons. This seems incredible, as Professor Wiehn has pointed out that we have more documentary evidence of the Holocaust than of any event in history. But of course psychology tells us that people have enormous capacities for self-deception. The Holocaust was, at any rate, carefully recorded by the National Socialists themselves. In Germany the denial of the Holocaust is called the Holocaust lie and propagating it is a punishable offense. Yet as long as people want to believe in falsehoods, it will be important to counter them with facts.

Further, even in accounts sympathetic to the victims, the Holocaust is often recreated in a distorted fashion. Popular films and TV shows may alter the story or characters in order to enhance their commercial appeal. There are versions created by ideologists for political purposes and to confirm their ideologies. Likewise, there are theorists who develop complex intellectual schemes, into which they attempt to force history. Of course we always start from a point of view in describing the past, which must always be recreated to be known. But an eyewitness account is one important corrective for the distortions introduced by artists, ideologists and theoreticians.

It often seems that the greatest amount of study is devoted to the famous and infamous. Just recently a lengthy and exhaustive book on Albert Speer was published dealing in excruciating detail with what he knew or did not know about the Holocaust and when. Don't we really know more than enough about such people? Is it not better to try, with Professor Wiehn and Dr. Jacques Stroumsa and others, to find out more about the ordinary people who, if they did not make momentous changes in history, at least tried to live decent lives and do some good for their families and those around them in the midst of troubled times and great suffering?

An autobiographical account such as this helps us to understand the personal experiences of the people who lived through the Holocaust. While there are historical works which present an overall picture on the basis of documents and statistical analysis, these works frequently leave out the personal dimension. This is important, because people do not experience history as an overall phenomenon, but rather live only in a particular limited segment of history. Especially in the case of the Holocaust, the personal experience is important. What novelist would ever imagine some of the bizarre incidents which are recounted by eyewitnesses such as Dr. Stroumsa, such as the hernia operation which he received in a modern, well-equipped operating room from a skilled surgeon? Such incidents have a Kafkaesque quality, occurring as they did in the midst of a death camp where Dr. Stroumsa could at any moment have been arbitrarily sent to the gas chambers or gunned down on some trivial pretext. Unexpected historical details like these must be written down to complete our record of the Holocaust. They help create a richer historical image and deepen our understanding of the strange workings of the totalitarian mind. Further, as Dr. Stroumsa points out, the attempt was made to keep the victims from using the media to learn what was happening in the world outside. And conversely, the outside world was to be prevented from knowing. Thus, for example, Chief Engineer Bosch and other people Dr. Stroumsa worked with while interned in the camps apparently did not know about the mass executions. Indeed, some inmates did not know crucial facts about what was happening around them, such as the rabbi whom no one had the heart to tell that his family had all been killed upon arrival.

As well, autobiographical accounts help us bridge the gap between our experiential worlds and those of the persons who lived in history. Of course we cannot expect to fully grasp their worlds. Dr. Stroumsa cites a proverb to the effect that those who went to Auschwitz can never return, and those who were not there can never go there. People sometimes exaggerate on their ability to see the world through the eyes of Holocaust survivors and victims, for example, in going so far as to identify their fate with that of Anne Frank or other admirable figures. Probably we cannot understand well enough to justify this sort of identification, but accounts such as the present one do add significantly to our understanding in ways that other forms of historical presentation cannot. The book could thus, for example, be read profitably as a supplementary text for courses on German and Jewish history.

The reader of a book on the Holocaust must also take into account a number of other cautionary notes. There has been a tendency in the last few years to relativize the Holocaust by applying the term and others, such as "genocide," as general terms for everything bad which is happening in our world. As Elie Wiesel recently stated,* "Banja Luka, Omarska and Srebrenica are places whose horrors should shock every human being who still believes in humanity. But they do not belong to the same kingdom of evil as Auschwitz. Auschwitz was and is different. Furthermore, Auschwitz remains unique in recorded history. Auschwitz meant the annihilation of an entire people: the last child, the last parent, the last soul was doomed." The Holocaust was focused chiefly at the total destruction of a single religious group, although of course not all victims were Jewish, and was systematically planned and technologically carried out on a scale and with a degree of effectiveness which other cases of mass murder do not approach. And this at a time when the technology was much less developed

---

* "Bosnia and the Holocaust." In: *Time*, August 7, 1995, p. 19.

than today. Thus we should be careful in drawing analogies between the incidents in this book and contemporary events, however evil they may be.

We should also be cautious about finding an inspirational message in this and other books about the Holocaust. The reader of this book will surely be moved to tears of sympathy at certain passages. But the emotion cannot be one of uplift, but rather of sadness. Some readers of books on the Holocaust and viewers of films such as *Shindler's List* or *The Diary of Anne Frank* apparently experience a sense of being uplifted by the positive human characteristics displayed by the protagonists or even of feeling good about being a human being.* There are, of course, inspiring moments in this book. For example, Dr. Stroumsa retains his humanity in Auschwitz. With his violin playing he even arouses sympathy in the cruel block guard, and he further uses his music to console sick comrades in the camp infirmary. Likewise, it is in many respects inspiring to see how he managed to rebuild his life afterwards. Chief Engineer Bosch's compassion for Dr. Stroumsa and other prisoners should also be remembered. However, the book contains many more references to inhumanity and injustice, for example, the cruelty of the guards upon the arrival in Auschwitz, the murder of Dr. Stroumsa's family and other people who appear in the story, such as David the technician, and the many evidences of the mass murders in the gas chambers at Auschwitz, the wretched, demeaning conditions under which the prisoners were forced to live and work, the horrendous death march to Mauthausen with people cold-bloodedly gunned down in the snow. These images of cruelty and inhumanity suggest that in reading about the Holocaust we should be less inspired by a sense of mankind's basic goodness than filled by a sense of pessimism about the potential evils in human nature, society and history and saddened by the senseless loss of life.

While there is no contemporary event which is the same as the Holocaust, there are groups in our society whose members glorify National Socialism and wish to revive it. Neo-nazi groups are active throughout the world. Thus recently an American Neo-Nazi was arrested in Denmark who had been sending quantities of virulent, fascist literature to Europe for years. Dr. Stroumsa's book and others in Professor Wiehn's series show concretely what these groups are glorifying and what they want to do. They show how many people, perhaps even ourselves, could be affected if they were to succeed. Thus these books help us to

---

* Cf. A.J. Rosenfeld, "The Americanization of the Holocaust." In: *Commentary*, Vol. 99, No. 6, 1995, pp. 35-40.

better understand the threat which such groups pose for our society. Hopefully, reading them will thereby increase our awareness of the need for vigilance.

Dr. Stroumsa is to be praised for reminding us once again more of the Holocaust and its personal meaning for victims and survivors. Today, when peace and good will seem so very possible and yet so very fragile, it is important to keep sight of the personal dimension of times when neither peace nor goodwill seemed at all possible. And it is important to honor people whose trials we will hopefully never have to endure. Professor Wiehn as well deserves a debt of gratitude for helping to ensure that readers in coming generations will have the opportunity to read this troubling story, and the stories of many other persons, victims of crimes whose memory must not be forgotten.

Konstanz, December 1995

Dr Jacques Stroumsa 1995 (photo Wiehn)

82

מסלוניקי לירושלים דרך אושוויץ ופריס

Appendix

Directors and teachers of the Jewish schools of Salonica (first from the right in the second row father Abraham Stroumsa)

Jacques Stroumsa (left) with his brother Guy (right) on the terrace of their parent's house in Salonica 1937; in the middle David Perahia, Julie's fiancée

The family Stroumsa on the terrace of their house (from the left) Julie, the mother, Bella, Guy (behind), the father, and Jacques as soldier 1937

Julie Stroumsa 1937

Moshe Safdie Memorial of Deportation in Yad Vashem, Jerusalem 1995 (photo Wiehn)

March 31st, 1943.

Ch. BARLAS, Esq.
c/o Dr. J. Goldin,
Kontinental Oteli,
Istanbul-Beyoglu

Dear Mr. Barlas,

I am sending you copy of a letter which I have received from a Sephardi Jew in Lausanne (I do not wish to give the name in writing). The report about the situation in Bulgaria and in the parts of Greece occupied by Bulgaria seems to be exact and has been confirmed to me by some other well-informed source. I suppose that you are in possession of all this information but in any case I wanted to let you have a copy of the report.

This throws also a light on certain reports you may have received in connection with the so-called Stadlan-business. You know from previous communications that I have no confidence in the sayings of certain Rabbanim. To make this business more attractive, it has been said that the famous Stadlan has arranged things in Greece in a favourable sense. I have had my doubts from the start but now it is more or less clear to me that all this is just "Schmuss". If you take a map and study the situation, you will see this :

The main part of Greece i.e. the Peloponneaus and the part north of the Gulf of Corinth is occupied by the Italians and you know that under Italian occupation no deportations have taken place.

Salonica is occupied by the Germans and nearly the whole population of Salonica has been evacuated long ago. Nobody knows what has become of the many Jewish inhabitants. Then there is a third part occupied by Bulgarian troops, namely the coastal zone between the Gulf of Orfano and Dedeagatsch. In the middle of this zone is Cavalla. Now this seems to be the part from which the deportations have lately taken place.

This being the position, I wonder who and where are the Greek Jews who have been so efficiently protected by Stadlan.

To complete the geographical picture it is to be noted that the German troops are also holding a corridor between the Turkish and Bulgarian frontier which now runs down through the former Greek territory (by the way this is one of the reasons why I do not believe in emigration from Italy through the neighbouring countries and then through Bulgaria to Istanbul; it may be different if your plans regarding a boat from Dedeagatsch will materialise but even then the risks and difficulties for people coming from Italy are greater than the chances to get them through).

I hope that these various bits of information will be of interest to you and I also hope that you will keep me informed from your side about these and other questions. It seems that Posner has some information concerning 25,000 certificates but I have not heard anything, at least not officially.

With kind regards

In: H. Friedlander/S. Milton (Gen. Ed.), Archives of the Holocaust, Vol. 4, New York, London 1990, p. 101

הרשימה לפי מספרי התובלה

1.	2.	3.	4.	5.	6.	7.	8.	9.	10.
1	20.3.1943	סאלוניקי	2800	109371—109787	417	38721—38912	192	609	2191
2	24.3.1943	סאלוניקי	2800	109896—110479	584	38962—39191	230	814	1986
3	25.3.1943	סאלוניקי	1901	110483—110941	459	39193—39428	236	695	1206
4	30.3.1943	סאלוניקי	2501	111147—111458	312	39632—39763	141	453	2048
5	3.4.1943	סאלוניקי	2800	112307—112540	334	39964—40221	258	592	2208
6	9.4.1943	סאלוניקי	2500	112974—113291	318	40280—40440	161	479	2021
7	10.4.1943	סאלוניקי	2750	114094—114630	537	40537—40782	246	783	1967
8	13.4.1943	סאלוניקי	2800	114875—115374	500	40841—41204	364	864	1936
9	17.4.1943	סאלוניקי	3000	115848—116314	467	41354—41615	262	729	2271
10	18.4.1943	סאלוניקי	2501	116317—116676	360	41616—41860	245	605	1896
11	22.4.1943	סאלוניקי	2800	117199—17453	255	42038—42250	413	668	2132
12	26.4.1943	סאלוניקי	2700	118425—118869	445	42882—43074	193	638	2062
13	28.4.1943	סאלוניקי	3070	118888—119067	180	43123—43483	361	541	2529
14	4.5.1943	סאלוניקי	2930	119781—120090	220	43779—44096	318	538	2392
15	7.5.1943	סאלוניקי	1000	—	—	44259—44326	68	68	932
16	8.5.1943	סאלוניקי	2500	120650—121217	568	44380—44626	247	815	1685
17	16.5.1943	סאלוניקי	4500	121910—122375	466	44931—45114	211	677	3823
18	8.6.1943	סאלוניקי	880	124325—124544	220	45995—46082	88	308	572
19	18.8.1943	סאלוניקי	1800	136919—137189	271	—	—	271	1529
20	11.4.1944	אתונה	1500	182440—182789	320	—	113	433	1067
21	30.6.1944	קורפו ויאנינה	2000	15229—15674	446	8282—8412	131	577	1423
22	16.8.1944	רודוס ואחרים	2500	7159—7504	346	24215—24468	254	600	1900
		סך הכל	54533		8025		4732	12757	41776
1.	2.	3.	4.	5.	6.	7.	8.	9.	10.

1. Transportation numbers; 2. Date of arrival in Auschwitz; 3. (Place of origin) Salonica; 4. number of deportees; 5. Concentration camp numbers of the men; 6. Number of men, who were not immediately sent to the gas chambers; 7. Concentration camp numbers of the women; 8. Numbers of women, who were not immediately sent to the gas chambers; 9. Total number of men and women, who were not immediately sent to the gas chambers; 10. Numbers of those, who were sent immediately to the gas chambers.

Konzentrationslager Auschwitz Art der Haft: _____ Gef. Nr. _____

(3034)

Name und Vorname: __Strumza, Macaues, Israel__

geb.: __4.1.13__ zu: __Saloniki__

Wohnort: __Saloniki, Erzsomenou 15__

Beruf: __Ziekhbauingenieur__ Rel.: __mos__

Staatsangehörigkeit: __Griechenland__ Stand: __verh.__

Name der Eltern: __Abraham u. Doudoun geb.__ Rasse: __jüd.__

Wohnort: __K.L. Au__

Name der Ehefrau: __Nora geb. Mordoh__ Rasse: __jüd.__

Wohnort: __K.L. Au__

Kinder: __—__ Alleiniger Ernährer der Familie oder der Eltern: _____

Vorbildung: __6 Kl. gr. Volkssch., 6 Kl. Gymn., 4 J. Univ. (Paris)__

Militärdienstzeit: __50. gr. Inf. Reg. Saloniki__ von – bis __1935__

Kriegsdienstzeit: __dto__ von – bis __1940-41__

Grösse: __158__ Nase: __w. gebogen__ Haare: __d. blond__ Gestalt: __mittel__

Mund: __norm__ Bart: __keinen__ Gesicht: __oval__ Ohren: __norm__

Sprache: __gr. span. fr. ital.__ Augen: __blau__ Zähne: __4 fehlen__

Ansteckende Krankheiten oder Gebrechen: __keine__

Besondere Kennzeichen: __keine__

Rentenempfänger: __nein !__

Verhaftet am: __30.4.43__ wo: __Saloniki__

1. Mal eingeliefert: __9.5.43__ 2. Mal eingeliefert: _____

Einweisende Dienststelle: __RSHA IV B 10 2125/43 (448)__

Grund: _____

Parteizugehörigkeit: __keine__ von—bis _____

Welche Funktionen: __keine__

Mitglied v. Unterorganisationen: __keine__

Kriminelle Vorstrafen: __ang. keine__

Politische Vorstrafen: __ang. keine__

Ich bin darauf hingewiesen worden, dass meine Bestrafung wegen intellektueller Urkundenfälschung erfolgt, wenn sich die obigen Angaben als falsch erweisen sollten.

v. g. u.   Der Lagerkommandant KL.-Au.
                                                        i. A.

Dr. Jaques Stroumsa in Auschwitz 1993

Auschwitz I 1983 (photo Wiehn)

Auschwitz II-Birkenau 1983 (photo Wiehn)

Dr. J.Goldin   Istanbul, 19.10.43.

C o n f i d e n t i a l

To: The Jewish Agency for Palestine,Immigration Dept.,Jerusalem
From: Dr. J.Goldin, Istanbul.

On Oct. 3rd the news reached us that the German authorities
have decided to deport the Jewish population of Athens. We then
approached the Greek authorities here with the request that an
appeal should be made through the Greek unofficial radio and other
active factors in Greece, and in the Greek population to help the
Jews, either in enabling the to escape from the concentration
centres in Athens and on their way of being deported to Poland,
or to assist them in every way, should they succeed in escaping.

Mr. K., first Secretary to the Greek Embassy, to whom
we appealed, readily agreed with our suggestions, which he trans-
mitted to his Ambassador by wire on the same day, with the request
to inform the Greek Government in Cairo.

On Friday Oct. 15th we were informed by Mr. K. that on
the 14th of the same month, at 11.5 p.m., during the Greek Hour,
the B.B.C.London broadcasted an appeal in Greek to the population,
to do everything in their power in order to help the co-nationals
of Jewish faith, who had so bravely fought at their side for the
freedom of their country. There is no doubt, the message continued,
that the Greek population would fulfil its duty towards the Jewish
patriots and further urged the sabotage of all anti-Jewish measures
taken by the Germans.

On the same day, Friday Oct. 15th, Mr. K. informed us
that he had received a wire from his Government, confirming the
receipt of his own wire and stating that the necessary instructions had been issued, in accordance with Mr. K's proposals, as
mentioned above.

                                    Yours faithfully,

P.S.: We have just received your wire of the 8th inst.,to which
       we have immediately replied. We reiterate that the person
       mentioned by you as "ESCOHE" or "ETCOHE" is unknown to us;
       we have no idea as to his identity.

In: H. Friedlander/S. Milton (Gen. Ed.), Archives of the Holocaust, Vol. 4, New York, London 1990, pp. 114

The wall of execution in Auschwitz I 1993 (photo Wiehn)

98

Konzentrationslager Auschwitz
Kommandantur/Abt. II

Auschwitz, den 16.Februar 1944.

Vernehmungsniederschrift.
===================================

Vorgeführt erscheint der Schutzh. Jude Nr. 121097 S t r u m s e r Jakob, geb. am 4.1.13 zu Salonicki und macht auf Befragen und zur Wahrheit ermahnt folgende Angaben zur S a c h e :

Ich bin im Büro der Unionwerke beschäftigt. Zwischen 16.00 und 18.00 Uhr arbeiten wir ebenfalls in den Werkhallen, wo ein Raum für uns vorgesehen ist, weil die grosse Postenkette zu dieser Zeit nicht mehr steht. Morgens nach dem Eintreffen in den Hallen gehen die im Büro beschäftigten Häftlinge ohne Begleitung in die Büroräume, welche ausserhalb des Zaunes liegen, hinüber. Am Montag, den 14.2.44 ging ich allein und etwas später von der Halle ins Büro, weil ich einige Bücher vergessen hatte und ausserdem mit dem Meister Fischer über einen Vorschlag sprechen wollte. Auf dem Wege zum Büro sah ich von weitem das sogenannte "Rotkäppchen-Kommando" der Häftlingsfrauen. Ich wusste von früher, dass meine Schwester Bella Strumser diesem Kommando angehört. Da ich sie bereits einige Male gesehen hatte. Ich wollte ihr zuwinken und ging deswegen einige Schritte vom geraden Wege ab. Hierbei wurde ich von einem SS-Rottenführer festgehalten, der mir Fluchtabsichten vorwarf.

Bei der Durchsuchung fand der SS-Rottenführer einen Zettel mit einer polnischen Adresse bei mir. Dieses ist die Adresse eines Häftlings, mit dem ich eng befreundet bin und mit dem ich nach einer eventl. Entlassung weiterhin in Verbindung bleiben wollte. ./.

Ich habe die Wahrheit gesagt und nichts verschwiegen.

v. g. u.

Geschlossen:

[Unterschrift]

SS-Unterscharführer

Vermerk:

Da S t r u m s e r Fluchtabsichten nicht einwandfrei nachgewiesen werden konnten, wurde keine Strafmeldung erstellt.

SITUATION OF THE JEWS IN OCCUPIED GREECE

1.- The Jewish population affected by the deportation to Poland, carried out by the german authorities in Greece, exactly one year ago, amounts to 60.000 which is roughly 3/4 of the entire Jewish pre-war population of Greece. They were chiefly the Jews from Salonika (55.000) and those living in the smaller communities of Macedonia and Thrace : i.e. Langada, Verria, Niaoussa, Florina, Sèrres, Drama, Cavalla, Xanthie, Komotini (Grommoultzina) Alexandroupolis (Dédéagatche) Dimotika, Horestial, Soufli.

2.- The Jews of the following nationalities : Italian, Spanish, Swiss, Turkish, Iranian, British and American, have been exempted of deportation to Poland, which measure applied to Greek Jews. Jews of other nationality did not exceed 1.000.Of the Greek Jews, those who were able to escape in the hills and who joined the guerilleros, as well as those who joined other parts of the country (mainly Athens), do not probably exceed 4.000.- There are serious reasons to fear that most of those who were shifted to Poland in sealed railway trucks (horse carriages) were exterminated when they ultimately reached their destination.

3.- Following the Italian collapse, early in October 1943, the german authorities endeavoured to put into force , in Athens and the rest of Greece (which was, so far, under italian administration) the same anti-jewish measures as in Salonica six months earlier. But, thanks to the acquired experience, the valuable help and assistance of the Orthodox Church, of all classes of the Christian population and of the different organizations of partisans, and also, owing to their restricted number the immense majority of the Athenian jews numbering then, about 8.000, found refuge in Christian houses, where they are hidden under false christian identities. Only a very small number of them were able to escape in the Middle East. With regard to the Jews of small provincial towns, they joined the partisans and they are sharing their fate, including women and children.

4.- The order issued by the German Military command in October last in Athens, stated that all Jews who would be caught after the expiry of an interval of 5 days given for their registration, would be shot and the christians who, by any means, would help them, would be sent into concentration camps. A further order, more recent, extends the death penalty to Christians who hide Jews. A concentration camp has been settled in the surroundings of Athens where numerous Jews who were recently caught as well as some who have been compelled to surrender themselves spontaneously, within the last 6 months, are being sent. It is considered unlikely that any of them will survive the ill-treatment implied.

./.

In: H. Friedlander/S. Milton (Gen. Ed.), Archives of the Holocaust, Vol. 4, New York, London 1990, p. 184

- 2 -

5.- The greatest risk sustained by the Athenian Jews remains in the intensification of the hunting which may at any moment be ordered by the Gestapo, which would easily lead to their capture. Besides, whilst the liberation of Greece is not as rapid as one would have expected in last October, there are serious reasons to believe that the moral of all the Jews who hide themselves decreases at the same time as their resources are being exhausted.

6.- If consideration is given to help efficiently Jews in Athens, it is not sufficient to extend their means of escaping by sea (whose results were very meagre so far). It is essential to send as soon as possible funds and, above all, to see that these funds are properly distributed. One must bear in mind, that in this final stage, all the Jews who will be caught, will have been lost on account of their lack of financial means. As regards Jews from provincial towns, who have joined the partisans in the hills, they must be helped by the regular expedition of funds, foodstuffs and medicines. It is reckoned that bout 20/25.000 Jews still live in Greece.

Cairo, 16th of April 1944.

UNITED STATES
HOLOCAUST MEMORIAL MUSEUM

Selected Literature

J. Adler et al., „The Last Days of Auschwitz." In: Newsweek, January 16, 1995, pp. 14-31.

Ph. Anty u. R. Clogg (Ed.), British Policy Towards Wartime Resistence in Yugoslavia and Greece. London 1975.

G. Baum, Die letzten Tage von Mauthausen. Berlin (Ost) 1965.

A. Barnea, Goral Echad. Jerusalem 1986 (Hebrew).

Y. Ben, Greec Jewry in the Holocaust and the Resistence 1941-1944. Institute of the Saloniki Jewry Research Center. Tel Aviv 1985 (Hebrew).

S. Bowman, "Jews in Wartime Greece." In: M.R. Maurus (Ed.), The Nazi Holocaust. Vol.4, Westport/London 1989, pp. 297-314.

U. Büttner (Hg.), Die Deutschen und die Judenverfolgung im Dritten Reich. Hamburg 1992.

G.F. Cashman, „Surviver of Auschwitz Orchestra to play at March of the Living." In: Jerusalem Post, March 31, 1994.

D. Czech, Kalendarium der Ereignisse im Konzentrationslager Auschwitz-Birkenau 1939-1945. Reinbek/Frankfurt 1989.

E. Demant (Hg.), Auschwitz - "Direkt von der Rampe weg..." Kaduk, Erber, Klehr: Drei Täter geben zu Protokoll. Reinbek 1979.

N. Eck, "New Light on the Charges against the last Chief Rabbi of Salonica." In: Yad Vashem Bulletin, Nr. 17, December 1965, pp. 9-16; Nr. 19, 1966, pp. 28-39.

F. Fénelon, Das Mädchenorchester in Auschwitz. (1976) München 1981.

H. Fleischer, Im Kreuzschatten der Mächte. Griechenland 1941-1944. Frankfurt a. M. 1977/87.

H. Friedlander/S. Milton, Archives of the Holocaust. Vol. 4, ed. by F.R. Nicosia. New York/London 1990.

P. Friedman, „The Jews of Greece during the Second World War. A bibliographical survey. In: Jewish Social Studies 5, 1953.

M. Gilbert, The Holocaust. A. History of the Jews of Europe during the Second World War. New York 1966.

R. Hilberg, Die Vernichtung der europäischen Juden. (1961) 3 volumes, Frankfurt a.M. 1990.

R. Hilberg, Täter, Opfer, Zuschauer. Die Vernichtung der Juden 1933-1945. Frankfurt a.M. 1992.

J.L. Hondros, Ocupation and Resistance. The Greek agony 1941-1944. New York 1983.

I. Kabeli, „The Resistance of the Greek Jews." In: YIVO Annual 8, 1953.

A. Kedros, La résistance Greque 1940-1944. Paris 1966.

E. Kolb, Bergen-Belsen 1943-1945. Göttingen 1985.

E. Kunio-Amariglio, Damit es die ganze Welt erfährt - Von Saloniki nach Auschwitz und zurück 1926-1996. Konstanz 1996 (in preparation).

H.S. Kounio, I Have Experienced Death. Saloniki 1982 (Greek)

H. Langbein, Menschen in Auschwitz. Wien 1972.

M. Molho (Hg.), In memoriam. Thessalonique 1973. - In memoriam - gewidmet dem Andenken an die jüdischen Opfer der Naziherrschaft in Griechenland. Essen 1981.

F. Müller, Sonderbehandlung. München 1979.

B. Naumann, Auschwitz. Bericht über die Strafsache gegen Mulka und andere vor dem Schwurgericht Frankfurt. Frankfurt 1965.

J. Nehama, Histoire des Israélites de Salonique. Tomes I-VII, Salonique 1935.

J. Piekalkiewicz, Krieg auf dem Balkan 1940-1945. München 1984.

G. Rabitsch, "Das KL Mauthausen." In: Studien zur Geschichte der Konzentrationslager. Schriftenreihe der Vierteljahreshefte für Zeitgeschichte, Nr. 21, Stuttgart 1971, pp. 50-92.

D. Recanati, Zikhron Saloniki. 2 Vol., Tel Aviv 5732 (Hebrew and Ladino).

G. Reitlinger, Die Endlösung. (1953/1956) 4. Auflage, Berlin 1961.

E. Sevillas, Athens - Auschwitz. Athen 1983

L. Shelley, Secretaries of Death. New York 1986.

W. Sofsky, Die Ordnung des Terrors: Das Konzentrationslager. Frankfurt a.M. 1993.

J. Tsatsos, Grèce 1941-1944. Journal de l'Occupation. Neuchatel 1967.

„Zeitsprung 1942-1995", in: ZEIT-Magazin (Hamburg), No. 14, March 31, 1995, pp. 8-9.

Editor

Dr.Dr.h.c. Erhard Roy Wiehn, M.A.

Professor of Sociology, University of Konstanz, Germany; publications mainly on Shoáh and Jewish Studies.

Jewish Fates in and from Greece edited by Erhard Roy Wiehn

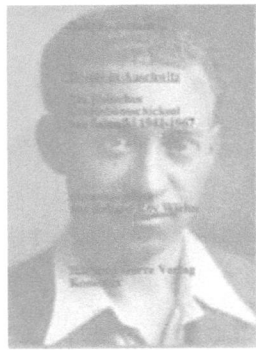

Jacques Stroumsa,
Geiger in Auschwitz
Ein jüdisches Überlebensschicksal
aus Saloniki 1941–1967.
Aus dem Französischen von Brigitte Pimpl
Konstanz 1993, 108 Seiten, Fotos, € 15,24.
ISBN 3-89191-652-3

Erika Myriam Kounio-Amariglio,
Damit es die ganze Welt erfährt –
Von Saloniki nach Auschwitz
und zurück 1926-1996.
2. Auflage 2003, 1996, 171 Seiten. € 19,80.
ISBN 3-89649-003-6

Erhard Roy Wiehn
Juden in Thessaloniki –
Die alte sephardische Metropole im kurzen his-
torischen Überblick
unter besonderer Berücksichtigung der Schoáh
1941-1944.
2. überarbeitete Aufl. 2018, 60 Seiten, 14,80
€. ISBN 978-3-86628-498-2

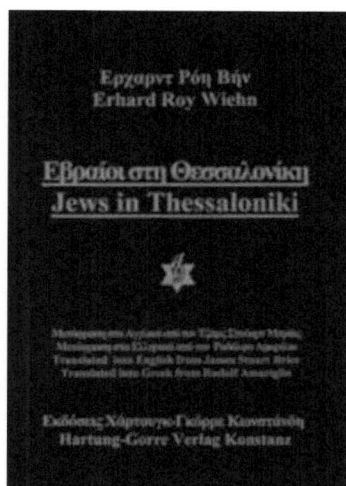

Erhard Roy Wiehn,
Ewräi sti Thessaloniki -
<u>**Jews in Thessaloniki**</u>.
(ins Griechische übertragen von
Rudolf Amariglio,
translated into English from
James Stuart Brice).

1st edition 2004. 74 pages, € 12,-.
ISBN 3-89649-909-2

Konrad Goerg
We are what we remember
Germans, Two Generations after Auschwitz
Voices to Remind Us
In Remembrance of Erwin Katz
Forewords by Horst Eberhard Richter
and by Erhard Roy Wiehn

1st Edition 2010 as Paperbook. 116 pages,
€ 9.95. ISBN 978-3-86628-342-8

1st Edition 2010 as ebook. US $ 9.15
on www.amazon.com
ISBN 978-3-86628-355-8

„Was aufgeschrieben, veröffentlicht und in einigen Bibliotheken der Welt aufgehoben ist,
wird vielleicht nicht so schnell vergessen." (Erhard Roy Wiehn)